SUICIDE

SUICIDE

By
Karen Ober Savalan - Author of
Midpoint Interpretation Simplified
Midpoint Synastry Simplified
Midpoint Love Simplified
Love Anger
Karen's Keyword Compendium

1st Edition

Second Printing 1983

Library of Congress, Cataglog Card # 82-61095

Published by
The American Federation of Astrologers, Inc.
P.O. Box 22040
Tempe, AZ 85282

Suicide

CONTENTS

PREFACE

To all of my readers who have experienced the agony of a great personal loss.... and to those who are coping with the element of suicide in some way in their lives I offer you my efforts in my latest work entitled, 'SUICIDE'.

Hopefully this book will serve as a catalyst making possible a three-fold benefit for you:

[l.] <u>HEALING</u>
For the survivors - A unique release from your eternity of isolated suffering, aching heart and quiet desperation over your loss - freedom from guilt!

[2.] <u>HELPING</u>
Preventing a tragedy through the development of a 'new awareness'!

[3.] <u>EXPLAINING FROM RESEARCH</u>
For those who want to fully understand the dynamics of astrological depression as well as for those who secretly ask the question, "Could this ever happen to me? This question will be forever satisfied through this book!

SELF HELP BOOKS

MIDPOINT INTERPRETATION SIMPLIFIED
By Karen Ober Savalan, D.F.Astrol.S.
Accurate interpretation plus professional future forecasting! Lib. of Congress Cat. Card #80-127755

MIDPOINT SYNASTRY SIMPLIFIED
By Karen Ober Savalan, D.F.Astrol.S.
Astounding discoveries plus control in all your relationships! Lib. of Congress Cat. Card #80-127803

MIDPOINT LOVE SIMPLIFIED
By Karen Ober Savalan, D.F.Astrol.S.
Opportunity to uncover your own unique love pattern plus a way to find or create your ideal lovemate! Lib. of Congress Cat. Card #80-69069

LOVE-ANGER
By Karen Ober Savalan, D.F.Astrol.S.
Emotional happiness and physical health by understanding and controlling your own mental love-anger energy! Lib. of Congress Cat. Card #81-65749

KAREN'S KEYWORD COMPENDIUM
By Karen Ober Savalan, D.F.Astrol.S.
Unique keyword approach that provides complete natal, synastry and future interpretation!
Lib. of Congress Cat. Card #81-69706

CHAPTER I

LETHAL MARS ENERGY PATTERN!

Prevent a crisis! Promote a change!

A bright, young 27 year old man made a frantic phone call to his lover seeking some emotional comfort. His pleas for solace went unrecognized as had many of his warning signals the during the weeks previous to his attempt. [See "Suicide Signals" - Page 35].

She was annoyed with his depression; the hour was late. John was just babying himself too much. She hung up on him; not from lack of love, but from lack of 'awareness' of the fateful drama that was about to take place.

The click was loud in his ears. He slowly put the phone back on the cradle. Then he calmly walked to the bathroom and opened up the medicine cabinet.

It was his intensely sensitive and repressed Scorpio Ascendant that took out a bottle of Seconal, filled a plastic cup with water and swallowed several handfuls of the bright orange capsules.

Then, with Capricorn Sun deliberateness, he sat down and wrote a long note telling her how much he loved her and how very tired he was from trying to cope with life.

The last year, as you will see through the directions and transits, had held much agonizing trauma for him.

His devotional Scorpio nature continued in the note to give definite instructions as to which dear friends and colleagues were to receive his prized possessions: his valuable record collection, his pictures, his precious memorabilia.

Duty-bound Capricorn Sun with the sensitive Neptune contact prompted him to give some last-minute encouragement to several dear ones with their problems.

At the end of these instructions, he commented on how sleepy he was becoming; the pencil markings scrawled a little and then they stopped . . . his precious, vital, young life was over!

This was John's 2nd and final suicide attempt.

Tragedy inevitably leaves the remaining loved ones consumed with guilt. There are a thousand unanswered questions.

Hopefully, this book on SUICIDE will dissipate this condition of futility and despair.

The following chapter is the beginning of discovery of unique answers for you.

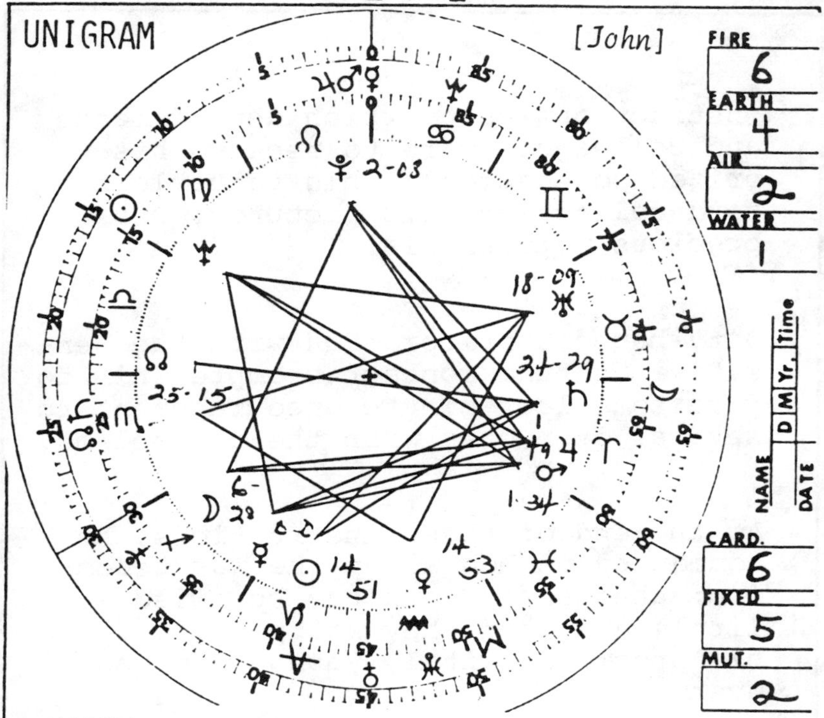

JOHN'S NATAL

CONFIDENTIAL FILE #1
ILLUSTRATION #1
JOHN'S NATAL CHART
MALE - JOHN

CARDINAL		
Mars in Aries	1 degree	34 minutes
Jupiter in Aries	1 degree	49 minutes
Saturn in Aries	24 degrees	29 minutes
Node in Libra	25 degrees	15 minutes
Sun in Capricorn	14 degrees	51 minutes
Mercury in Capricorn	0 degrees	0 minutes
FIXED		
Uranus in Taurus	18 degrees	09 minutes
Pluto in Leo	2 degrees	08 minutes
MC in Leo	20 degrees	35 minutes
Ascendant in Scorpio	11 degrees	36 minutes
Venus in Aquarius	14 degrees	53 minutes
MUTABLE		
Neptune in Virgo	25 degrees	29 minutes
Moon in Sagittarius	6 degrees	28 minutes

PART I
ANALYSIS OF THE SUBJECT

CONFIDENTIAL FILE #1
ILLUSTRATION #1
Felo-de-se [SELF DESTRUCT]
Dr. John Matthew Lyons - Male

He was 22 years old - going away to graduate school in a week on a scholarship. He watched a movie at about 8:00 P.M., didn't see it through to the end, and affectionately bid the family goodnight.

He gave his mother a peck on the cheek as he left the room, quietly went upstairs, took 30 Coricidin pills, and unsuccessfully attempted suicide for the first time.

To discover the 'why' of any suicide attempt it is necessary to check the directions a year or so previous to the attempt to see what was happening.

At that time, Directed Neptune was making contact with John's Natal Sun. This direction brought weakened health as well as identity confusion.

DIRECTIONS

THE YEAR OF THE SUICIDE ATTEMPT

The Natal Venus/Uranus love midpoint contacted by Directed Saturn-Node forced reality through love discussion. This contact indicates great psychological tension.

The love decision was made through the Directed Venus/Mercury-Mars-Jupiter group (opposition in the 90° circle) contacting the Natal Saturn-Node. This contact terminated the love relationship.

Love depression was heavy as Saturn's contact stripped away Neptune glamour and illusion midpoints in the natal Venus love structure. John was to experience love as a principle, not as an emotion. The planetary love picture is as follows:

VENUS

MOON.......	....SATURN
MOON.......	....NODE
MERCURY.......	....MARS
MERCURY.......	....JUPITER
MARS.......	....NEPTUNE
JUPITER.......	....NEPTUNE
URANUS.......	....ASCENDANT
ASCENDANT.......	....MC

INTERPRETATION OF THE NATAL VENUS LOVE STRUCTURE AS IT CONTACTS SATURN BY DIRECTION

KEYWORDS: [Transiting Saturn to...]

VE = MO/SA-NO	Reality emotions [Mo/Sa] want reality love [Ve/Sa]
VE = ME-MA-JU	Serious love [Sa/Ve/-Ma/Ju] discussions and communications [Me]
VE = MA/NE	With Saturn the love nature longs for enduring spiritual love. Ineffectively it becomes confused, erotic love [Ve/Ma/-Ne]
VE = JU/NE	With Saturn the love principle is philosophic [Jupiter] and spiritual [Neptune] - Ineffectively it can be dissatisfied expansion [Ju/Sa] of a false love concept [Ve/Ne]
VE = UR/ASC	Saturn brings psycho-

logical tension [Ur] forcing love [Ve] to move slowly with principle thus building an enduring love contact. With Saturn, Venus/Uranus/-Ascendant can no longer manifest ineffectively as a sudden/sexual/emotional love contact [Ve/Ur/Asc]

VE = ASC/MC — Stable [Sa] love outlook [Ve/Asc] involves the ego [MC] and the self esteem [MC]. This would involve John's rearing and family background. [Sa]

The above planetary contacts brought two very tragic events to John that year that would effect the course of his entire life.

A very dear friend and colleague committed suicide; she had been a uniquely loving and understanding platonic companion.

During that same year, John unfortunately fell deeply in love with a married woman which presented a devastating situation for him with his staunch religious background.

Directed Ascendant/MC midpoint contacting Natal Saturn-Node brought a great sense of depression and isolation into his relationships. Transiting Saturn to Natal Saturn-Node/MC deepened depression to despair.

It became virtually impossible for John to communicate. [Ascendant/MC/-Saturn/Node keywords would tell you that depression and inhibition tied in with the outlook, the ego and the relationships.

John's sister recalls going to his bedroom many times to talk with John as had been their custom.

There was a strange new quiet, paralyzed kind of climate between them now that had never been there before; they just could not pierce this inhibiting atmosphere to communicate. [Saturn to MC]

Once she just sat in the chair by the window for a long time almost as if she were subconsciously trying to force a break-through in communication.

The day was sunny and John had his

books and all the graduate school literature spread all over his bed, but he just stared out the window. When she finally did leave the bedroom he reached for her hand and said, "Thank you."

She responded with, "I love you," and felt some slight confidence that for the moment her presence had given him some small comfort.

John could not break the planetary barriers that prevented communication for him; his acute emotional agony grew.

The final blow that ignited the attempt came when John discovered that the woman he idolized, his sophisticated married lover, had several lovers besides John; one ironically being his best friend.

This was too much to bear!

TRANSITS FOR THE ATTEMPT

Transiting Saturn to the Natal Venus-Ascendant/Saturn-Node love contact was the catalyst that set off the Saturn Direction. [Saturn-Node to

Natal Venus/Uranus midpoint.] One stalked the other bringing emotional devastation and sudden separation from a female.

Transiting Mars to Natal Neptune/ Ascendant weakened the energy and emotionalized the outlook as well as two other midpoints: Uranus/Pluto and Sun/Moon. [Both these midpoints falling under the Neptune structure.]

Uranus/Pluto midpoint indicates a transformation. John's individuality was meant to grow and change.

Transiting Mars to Natal Neptune with its Sun/Moon [male/female] midpoint added emotional shock and torment to the chaotic Neptune=Uranus/Pluto upheaval.

The deception by his dear friend was possibly every bit as painful as the deception by his lover. The Aquarius Venus and the Sagittarian Moon placed great emphasis on friendship.

Fortunately transiting Jupiter contacted Saturn and its beneficial 'fortunate release' midpoint - Jupiter/Uranus - so John did not die.

He experienced the change of residence

that Jupiter/Saturn/Uranus meant for him; he went away to graduate school and a whole new way of life.

And John's family, though shaken and tormented by the suicide attempt, along with the complete inability to reach or give comfort to John, still received overwhelming benefits from life through John's Jupiter/Saturn/-Uranus.

They were permitted to have John for five more precious years of life!

John's first serious love affair was over. His sophisticated married lover divorced her husband and married one of her many, young, college-boy lovers.

And when John successfully committed suicide five years later she sent an incredibly beautiful white orchid dramatically enclosed in a lovely glass cylinder to sit by his coffin.

This gesture indicated the potential development of some feeling or some sensitivity in her make-up.

Her time spent with John did have a very lovely meaning when viewed through their possible growth.

She taught John the first great trauma he was to experience in love through his ineffective handling of his natal Venus square Uranus.

This was a great lesson, but unfortunately John did not learn it.

Five years later, John again attempted suicide taking an overdose of Seconal tablets. This time he succeeded! The newspaper report read as follows:

Newspaper Report

New York - Dr. John Matthew Lyons - 27 - former Pennsylvanian, who was Counseling Service Director and Assistant Professor of Psychology at the University of New York was found dead at his home Monday.

He was found by a Bell Telephone Company repairman. The repairman was there because of a trouble call on Lyons' phone line.

The Assistant to the Chancellor at the University was there to learn why he was not at school.

Police said Lyons was on the bedroom floor with the telephone under him. They said he apparently had taken an overdose of barbituates. He had been despondent and under the care of a physician. His home is in Pittsburgh, Pennsylvania.

JOHN'S NATAL INTERPRETATION

The balancing of power in John's chart involved the strategic channeling of an enormous amount of dynamic life force through a very impetuous, unrestrained Aries Mars with a sensitive, weakening Neptune contact!

[You will see how vital your own Mars energy thrust is as you perceive John's struggles.]

His Capricorn Sun with the Pluto contact [parallel] tells us he would by his very nature, over-tax his strength in his striving for leadership. Pluto allows no middle ground with its intensity, especially in difficult aspects; its fanatic drive for leadership brought with it cold, lonely isolation.

Pluto not only added an intense compulsiveness to the Capricorn Sun, but made it even more reserved, aloof and reclusive than Capricorn already is by his very nature.

John's commanding Capricorn Sun-Pluto and the strong, intense Saturn midpoint to the Sun/Pluto pulled him away from companionship in his youth and set him apart, creating a very structured life.

John held two jobs as a youngster, paperboy and clerk at a pharmacy. People many times his age came to him with their problems and his sensitive Neptune gave them comfort.

It was through these people, never through John, that the family heard so many of the kind and thoughtful things he had done for them.

Repression was emphasized through the stoical Sun/Pluto Capricorn and the Scorpio Ascendant with the enormous feeling capacity. John found it difficult to turn to anyone; he so strongly felt the Pluto compulsion to be 'a cut above the others.'

His mother often related with great pride of John's independence and self sufficiency as a youngster. He saved his money from working two jobs to return to his piano lessons; he insisted on paying for his own lessons, refusing the family's financial assistance.

The piano was a wonderful tool for John to release his intense, sensitive, pent-up Pluto feelings; he became an excellent pianist.

Paying for his own lessons was nothing more than the strong combination of Sun/Saturn/Pluto shown in the contact to the Sun as well as in the Saturn= Sun/Pluto midpoint. This along with the proud Scorpio Ascendant demanded he be his own man, completely in charge of his life.

The Capricorn Sun with the sensitive Neptune/Pluto midpoint gave John an individuality that was readily or excessively affected by external stimuli or influences; he was so easily hurt or offended.

This midpoint added to the already natural reclusiveness of the cool, aloof Capricorn and greatly increased his sense of isolation and made it so difficult to push out into the world.

Sun/Neptune/Pluto combination demands a moderate life and freedom from any escapism. Even medication will be a burden with this midpoint; the positive being of course the high spiritual evolvement that this contact offers.

Later, through Neptune illusion, John slipped into a pattern of chemical abuse thinking it a placebo offsetting the sensitivity and inhibition in his make-up.

John's very friendly Sagittarian Moon and his three enthusiastic planets in Aries [Mars/Jupiter/Saturn] with the Neptune charisma contact always easily gathered a large number of friends.

The relationships operating effectively were always the same; John was always a counselor to his peers. Sensible Saturn contacting Mars/-Jupiter teamwork with Neptune compassion and understanding was responsible for the following statement made by John.

He so eloquently spoke his chart in this regard in a letter to a very dear friend when he wrote, "I don't know why it is, but in all my relationships I am always needed, but never permitted to need!

John's Neptune contact to his Scorpio Ascendant was so sensitively acute, that without some 'aloneness time' to recharge, the Neptune contact could become a destructive force bringing confusion and insidious undermining to the outlook and the environment.

[You will see this happen about a year and a half before John's suicide.]

For hard-core strength you see two prominent midpoints that John made good use of.

Capricorn Sun midpointing Mars/Saturn indicated extremely hard work through very frustrated energy.

Jupiter/Saturn at the midpoint of the Capricorn was another hard-working combination. This midpoint normally indicates eventual career success, but only through painstaking progress. This is the well known 'one step forward, two steps backward' cement foundation building success promised by Jupiter/Saturn to the sun.

Unfortunately, both these midpoints could only be developed through extreme frustration and obstacles.

Career success must come for John through frustration [Mars/Saturn] along with depression and suicide thoughts [Jupiter/Saturn]. These are the obstacles that must be surpassed for career growth.

His touch of Uranus in the natal trine to the Sun gave John good progressive individuality, but when that same Uranus contacted natal Venus by square with an incredibly close orb of 3°-16", you see the touchy, disruptive influence in his relationships that added more frustration for the intense Scorpio Ascendant.

The love picture was not good; it would take enormous effort to stabilize it.

First, John's Venus in Aquarius was, by nature, a very independent lover. John could have many loves and feel a romantic attachment for each.

The lover would be his friend as well as his lover. Freedom in the relationship was paramount. When independent Venus in Aquarius squared super-independent Uranus you know that the emotional touchiness here is bound to cause many sudden ruptures in love.

Venus/Uranus can be in love today and indifferent tomorrow. Variety in love can become more important than maintaining one stable love relationship.

John was very depressed about his relationships as related by a friend. Shortly before his suicide, John had expressed concern over not being able to find security in one permanent love relationship.

The friend related one of John's quotes, "Even while I'm attempting to construct something permanent in a relationship, I'm destroying at the same time. So self defeating I am. This I know also. I really wonder if I'll ever be able to establish some lasting romantic relationship. I doubt it."

This was a unique example of John's Venus searching for stability or trying desperately to demand permanency from his love relationship with the Venus=Moon/Saturn midpoint. Love [Venus] and emotions [Moon] want stability [Saturn].

Moon/Venus/Saturn worked at offsetting the ineffective result of the highly magnetic, emotionally-intense sex energy from the Venus/Uranus square.

To further complicate the love picture, John's Mars in Aries was extremely impetuous. John had to work at controlling his impulses and enthusiasms. This discipline was the only way to sustain interest long enough to build something stable in a love relationship.

This Mars in Aries contacting Jupiter

in Aries in the 5th house of love gave an abundance of energy and enthusiasm for the enjoyment of life.

John would quite naturally pursue love and pleasure in a very aggressive emotional way in regard to his romantic laisons. The strong sexual drive in this Aries [5th house] combination possesses an urgency to find a love partner.

Lastly, in regard to the lovelife, the impulsive, unrestrained Mars/-Jupiter/Saturn in Aries could be weakened through Neptune. You see this combination in the following contacts:

90° Circle
Saturn [Natal Midpoint]

Venus...|....Mars/Jupiter

360° Circle
Mars opposition Neptune [6°-05"]
Jupiter opposition Neptune [6°-20"]

The saving grace would be the channeling of this intense Venus/Uranus romantic love imagination to some sort of artistic, creative outlet. To a point, this creative challenge was available in John's work.

There is always strength to offset the manifestation of ineffective contacts, but again, as stated earlier, even strength demands drawing lines.

John's Saturn which indicates the building of the character was so strongly aspected that without placing proper limits, John's Saturn energy became fanatic in the discipline area of his life [Sa=So/Pl]

Example: When John was put in charge of the psychology clinic in New York he permitted his work day to go to twelve hours a day; this eventually created a pattern that turned into depression!

Saturn in Aries midpointing the fanatic Sun/Pluto along with Neptune contacting the Scorpio Ascendant created the unrestrained idealist. John was going to save the world.

He saw his psychology development as a great mission in life. He said in a letter to a friend, "By the time I go down the hall to my office I have had at least five or six people turn to me with their problems."

This was indicative of the great healing power of Neptune's immediate warm sympathy - an effective environmental manifestation. This must have been truly rewarding for the great depth and enormous emotional strength of the very young, intense-loving Scorpio Ascendant.

The Achilles heel was, of course, the hairline between the missionary spirit of Neptune and the ego trip of the compulsive Pluto Capricorn Sun or the extremes of emotionalism and fanaticism generated by these combinations.

Returning to the second attempt and actual suicide, we again see the same Venus love structure making a contact to Saturn/Node.

This occurring, as before, over a year before the suicide tells us that there has been love discussion, along with a search for love and finding disappointment. There would again have been a love separation or separations.

The ego was burdened. A Saturn Direction to the ego filled it with depression and worry. [Directed Saturn to Natal MC.]

Saturn to the MC again made discussion very difficult, so not much was ever known as to why he seemed so overwhelmed with career failure when he seemingly was doing very well.

John vaguely discussed with a friend the possibility of relocating. There seemed to be some depression and dissatisfaction in what John felt his superiors expected from him.

John came home several months before his death. He seemed very happy, played the piano, laughed and socialized easily with the family and his friends, but his sister knew something was not right.

A week after he returned she wakened in the early morning distraught. Her husband found her sobbing in the kitchen. Her explanation was simply that John was going to die by the first of the year unless someone could reach him.

No amount of consolation relieved her and phone conversations with John did not bring anything to light. John insisted he was happy and content.

Less than two months later he killed himself.

The sudden change from depression to

happiness had been only false reassurance for John's family. A great weight had been lifted from his shoulders around the time of John's visit home; he had simply made the sub-conscious decision to die. [See Suicide Signals - Page 36]

To continue with the directions for the suicide: Directed Sun again had made a contact with Neptune. This time the Neptune condition was much more chaotic resulting from a decision John had made a year earlier.

When Transiting Neptune contacted the Ascendant [his outlook and environment] John made a decision that would eventually lead to his death. [He was also under the influence of a Neptune Direction at this time].

He opened the doors to Neptune exploitation. He made this decision thinking of himself as a great humanitarian, I am sure; his Neptune being so compassionate. As well as through a sense of personal loneliness and isolation [natal Sun/-Saturn/Pluto].

He could not help enough people at the clinic in his long, toilsome workday. His compassionate Neptune invited a few client friends to take refuge in his home until they were through their difficult times. This decision was the beginning of the subtle, insidious Neptune undermining of the outlook and the environment. [Ascendant].

It was a bad transformation [Sun/-Uranus/Pluto] made under a Neptune illusion. These client-patient relationships needed to be handled within the confines of his private office as Doctor/Client. [Saturn demands structured teamwork with Mercury/Venus/Mars/Jupiter].

His clients could, in no way, be helped through what John considered would be beneficial, loving teamwork-discussion in a comfortable home atmosphere.

What started out to be a great effort at healing the world turned into a nightmare of destructive relationships and chemical abuse.

As you watch the transits you see Neptune first contact John's outlook with subtle erosion. This was, of course, the Ascendant. Neptune permeated the environment.

Then, Neptune stalked the dangerous

midpoint path between the Ascendant and Venus and Uranus. John fell in love with several of his clients. The relationships that once were strong and clinical were now sexual and emotional.

Saturn lost! Neptune won! The game was over.

The effective, beneficial, imaginative Neptune faculty could no longer function at an intellectual level. Without Saturn, Neptune lost its limits and there was no one with structure to help John find his way again.

What he thought were sensitive, caring people were merely weak, parasitic misfits that had slipped into his home and eroded his character. [Character of course represented by natal Saturn contacts eroded through illusive Neptune Direction and Transit].

NOTE:
[At this point in the analysis, the author must speak to the effective manifestation of Neptune so that the readers are not biased from the above case study.

Many years of research as well as personal experience confirm to the author the Saturn energy necessary to build a strong, creative Neptune. Enormous effort must go toward channeling energy into patterns of discipline that build consistent routine and method; this effort must sometimes border on development past the point of being human.

This is the requirement for Neptune to be able to spew forth its great, creative accomplishments. Again, once acquired, such as in John's work, there is no guarantee that the individual can hold it. The only guarantee is continual work at the Saturn level of the chart!

Back to John's chart and the suicide year you see Uranus playing with Neptune and the Ascendant. Witte-Lefeldt in Rules For Planetary Pictures, called the situation with their interpretation, "To be involved by others through lack of understanding."

Ebertin, in his Combination of Stellar Influences, describes John's condition with, "The trait of succumbing to the influence of others easily - misfortune - to be hindered, harmed or defamed by others."

Where, then, was the cut-off point

for this young Scorpio's intense, caring nature to separate his needs from those of others?

Simplistically, it must begin and end with Saturn.

Transiting Pluto midpointing Venus/-Saturn called for a fateful separation or the rebuilding of a love relationship. The relationships did not have the quality to rebuild. John could not handle any more love torment in his life. He chose to die.

Mars midpointed his Moon/Neptune on the day of his death and his highly emotionalized feelings felt defeated and confused from the chaotic environment. He died in a home where just a bedroom away a few friends were sleeping off the effects of alcohol from the party the night before. Neptune was truly everywhere.

John had made his final Sun/Uranus/-Pluto transformation; he went to something better for himself.

SUMMARY
SUICIDE CONTACTS

Since it would take reams to analyze all of the contacts in any individual's chart we will summerize with some of the main suicidal configurations in John's chart:

[1.] Over-strained mentality - [Mercury in contact with Mars]

[2.] Creativity vs. Confusion - [Sun in relation to Neptune through the Sun = Neptune/Pluto midpoint

[3.] Element of desperation - [The Aries group - Mars, Jupiter and Saturn in Aries

[4.] Great excitability leading to self destruction - [Mars midpointing natal Ascendant - Venus/Uranus and MC]

NEPTUNE KEYWORD CONTACTS:

Neptune/Mercury
Creative or Confused Mentality

Neptune/Mars

Creative or Confused energy

Neptune/Jupiter
Creative or Confused Happiness

Neptune/Ascendant
Creative or Confused Outlook and Environment

Sun = Neptune/Pluto
Intensely Creative or Intensely Confused Individual

Moon = Venus/Neptune
Creative or Confused Love Emotions

Moon = Uranus/Neptune
Sudden Emotional Creativity or Sudden Emotional Confusion

Mercury = Mars/Neptune
Creative Mental Energy or Confused Mental Energy

Mercury = Jupiter/Neptune
Creative Mental Expansion or Chaotic Mental Expansion

Venus = Mars/Neptune
Spiritual Love Energy or Erotically Confused Love Energy

<u>Saturn = Neptune/MC</u>
Stable Ego and Goals in life or Depressed/Inhibited Ego and Goals in life.

<u>Neptune = Moon/Sun</u>
Spiritual Male/Female relationship
Disappointing Male/Female relationship

<u>Neptune = Uranus/Pluto</u>
Sensitive or Spiritual changes or transformations
Disappointing Transformations

<u>Neptune = Pluto/MC</u>
Spiritually intense Ego and Life Goals
Disappointment follows Fanatic or Confused Ego and Life Goals

<u>Pluto = Moon/Neptune</u>
Intense Emotions
Fanatic Emotions

<u>Ascendant = Mercury/Neptune</u>
Outlook that is Mentally Sensitive
Outlook that is Mentally Confused

<u>Ascendant = Mars/Neptune</u>
Outlook that is Energetically Sensitive or Spiritual
Outlook that is Energetically Impotent or Confused

MC = Sun/Neptune
Ego that is expressed Sensitively or Spiritually
Ego that is Confused

END of SUMMARY
SUICIDE CONTACTS

SUICIDE SIGNALS

[1.] Giving away prized possessions
John did this in his note under the influence of Saturn depression. This happens sometimes just before the actual attempt. [See John do this on page 2]

[2.] Talking and threatening to commit suicide
On the first attempt, Saturn depression denied John's communication of suicide to others. On the second and final attempt Neptune anxiety prompted John to speak of suicide often to his friends. [See Planetary Depression correlated with Saturn and Neptune - page 182]

[3.] Loss of humor over prolonged period of time
Transiting Saturn to John's MC had made life so serious and worrisome for John that his friends commented on John's lack of humor which ordinarily with the Sagittarian Moon and Aries/-Mars/Jupiter was always so much a part of all their get-togethers.

[4.] Loss of interest in life over prolonged period of time

Planetary influences here can be loss of interest in life from:

Saturn depression,
Uranus frustration,
Neptune anxiety, or...
Pluto isolation

See John exhibit this behavior on page 9]

[5.] Accident pattern - Something is going on in the subconscious that the person can't face

John had many car accidents a year prior to his final suicide attempt; this was the result of Neptune confusion as well as chemical abuse.

[6.] Sudden improvement when a person has been depressed for a long period of time can indicate the decision to commit suicide has been made

See the planetary influences under which John made this decision - page 25

END of
SUICIDE SIGNALS

HOW TO HANDLE PLANETARY STRESS

[1.] Think of what "you need and want first"
This can involve, in many cases, less acceptance of Saturn duty!

[2.] Forgive your errors - Perfection is for fools!
Neptune in difficult contact to your other planets can create this situation; you can sometimes feel unworthy or worthless if you are not perfect.

[3.] Decide realistically what must be accomplished each day
Saturn can give a good balance here. Uranus can be very innovative in creating good organization. Neptune demands routine and method. Pluto's intensity must combine a certain moderation in its nature for realistic daily accomplishment.

[4.] Accept your limitations!
Know your own chart in this regard. What are your limitations? Saturn can exact too much duty. Uranus sometimes throws away too quickly. Neptune dreams too big and becomes confused. Pluto becomes reclusive; goes into hiding too fast. List your planetary contacts on a sheet of

paper and discover what pushes you too hard and what holds you back.

[5.] Placing limits

By this point in the reading, you will have effectively made the following decisions in regard to your make-up:

[1.] Made the decision as to what you need and want out of life.
[2.] Made the decision to forgive your errors.
[3.] Made the decision to opt for only realistic daily accomplishment.
[4.] Made the decision to accept your limitations knowing what these limitations are.

NOW you must consistently place limits so that you can maintain this effective program of anti-stress for you. Others, even loved ones, will undermine these resolutions if you let them!

[6.] Bring the creative factor into your life

Since Neptune represents creative energy, you must learn to use the effective Neptune avenues to circumvent stress from entering your life. Neptune can serve as the perfect tranquilizer to combat stress through its love of music, writing, singing, dancing, the arts in general.

[7.] Work off tension - A physical activity program of some kind to offset tension

Every chart needs different tension outlets or types of exercise. An Aries fire sign will thoroughly enjoy and benefit from jogging where a Pisces water sign will find ballet a more suitable tension outlet. Determine your astrological needs before you set up a good physical activity program.

[8.] Sleep

When sleep becomes a problem, 'use' the planetary influences in your chart to offset the insomnia.

Saturn forces intellectual development through insomnia resulting from depression. Don't take tranquilizers - Read, during insomnia periods, and move forward in life as a result! Uranus helps you to discover unique ways in which you can change yourself and your environment. These changes can all come as result of disturbance of the sleep pattern; you are forced to diversify.

Sleeplessness can bring Neptune creativity; with Neptune this period also demands more tone with the body. A program of mild exercises helps here. Spiritual development now becomes important.

You re-create through Pluto when your sleep pattern is disrupted. Insomnia can force you to re-evaluate your life patterns and goals. It is an opportunity to discard what is obsolete and no longer workable.

[9.] Medication - This includes sedatives and tranquilizers
There will be times when medication is beneficial, but only in moderation and for a limited period of time.

A chart with many Neptune contacts will always have to place more limits with medication than another chart.

Any obstacle can be dissipated, overcome, or used for your benefit if you take the time to learn to manipulate the planet's energies!

END of
HOW TO HANDLE PLANETARY STRESS

CHAPTER II

SYNASTRY - CHART COMPARISON

John and His Sister

Unfortunately, we are not as unique as we would like to believe we are. In our joys as well as in our sorrows we react, in certain similar ways, as do hundreds of others experiencing the same emotional event.

Definite stages of emotional suffering, that we experience as a result of adjusting to and accepting the inevitability of the loss of a loved one, are prevalent in every tragic case.

These stages apply not only to suicide, but to any vital, agonizing love rejection.

The following stages tie in with directions and transits igniting an individual's natal planetary chart. The stages along with their general planetary influence are:

[1.] <u>GUILT - SATURN</u>
Guilt is a feeling of responsibility for some real or imagined offense. Saturn is usually at the basis of guilt.

[2.] <u>ANGER or RAGE - MARS/PLUTO</u>
<u>ARIES/SCORPIO</u>
Anger is a strong feeling of displeasure or belligerance, represented by Mars. Rage is intense anger bordering on fury and violence represented by Pluto.

[3.] DEPRESSION - SATURN - CAPRICORN
Depression is anger turned inward. It is basically a Saturn emotional reaction characterized by feelings of sadness, loneliness, rejection, etc. [Depression can also come from Uranus frustration - Neptune anxiety or Pluto isolation]

[4.] DENIAL - NEPTUNE [and SATURN]
Denial is behavior manifesting as a rejection of reality. Neptune denies reality by building fantasy. Saturn can be very life-denying by accepting too much self discipline.

[5.] ISOLATION - PLUTO [and SATURN]
Isolation behavior manifests as withdrawal or separation; to be alone.

[6.] ACCEPTANCE AND BARGAINING
Bargaining can be part of an adjustment that precludes love rejections [Venus/Saturn] from ever happening again. Example would be an individual who finds love in a universal way, through altruistic group work, versus seeking love in a one-to-one relationship where the threat of rejection is stronger.

The following confidential synastry narration will have sprinkled throughout its story of love-loss, certain definite manifestations of Saturn despair, Uranus frustration, Neptune anxiety and Pluto isolation. Some influences being, of course, more predominate than others.

To gain the most personal benefit from this section on Synastry recall a tragic love experience you have encountered. Then note, not only your behavior reactions, but the planetary keywords that manifested the strongest during this period in your life.

PLANETARY KEYWORDS

SATURN......DESPAIR
URANUS......FRUSTRATION
NEPTUNE.....ANXIETY
PLUTO.......ISOLATION

This keyword reference will help you discover something unique in regard to your chart; it will point up the strongest planetary influence operating during your personal love-loss tragedy.

This knowledge can serve as a great, intellectual safeguard against ever debilitating yourself through future planetary directions and transits.

A STAR * is placed beside each different stage of emotional suffering to stress the universality of the grief-recovery stages in every case of tragic loss. It is well to note that these stages do not follow in any particular order.

GUILT *

[Directed Saturn to John's sister's natal Ascendant brought guilt, depression and discipline; all Saturn qualities you will see manifest.

His death left her with not only enormous guilt, but equally as devastating doubts and uncertainties about the relationship.

Did he ever really love her? Or, was she just a family member that he tolerated and was, in essence, quite a chore for him? Did she ever give him any comfort; was she unique or of value in some small way to him?

Questions similar to the above have plagued, not only John's sister - but millions of people in relationships where they have been suddenly abandoned; left numb and grief stricken with loss, searching for some value in what they felt was a unique togetherness.

The resulting emotional vacuum emerging from the absence and denial of the very-valued loved one demands an answer. Not only for personal comfort, but more important, for the therapeutic healing that must take place in order to bridge the gap to the successful forming of another love relationship.

If this transformation does not occur, then a rejected love relationship can be viewed through confused emotionalism and seen as something dangerous and futile; the underlying, bewildered, suppressed emotions saying, "To love is too risky; it inevitably brings loss."

The quiet calm that can end this tormenting analyzation and questioning can come only through a superior intellectual tool; no amount of emotional persuasion can mask this torture born of the mind not of the emotions.

Synastry is this intellectual tool. Synastry is the study of relationships. It is a scientific comparison of two birth charts or of two horoscopes.

This comparison can find unique answers explaining the interaction between people. Through the study of synastry, answers emerge that can finally lay to rest the torment created from the loss of love.

It can be your release as it was John's sister's. Experience now the rewards of this unique synastry tool as you listen in on the Astrological Consultation between the Astrologer and his client, John's sister:

CONSULTATION

[As related by the Astrological Consultant]

When my client, John's sister spoke of him, you could feel the strength of her possessive Capricorn Venus contacted by intense Pluto.

She spoke of John in the present tense as if he were still with her. Although the loss occurred years ago there was still a need for astrological answers as to the relationship they shared - a closeness so unique that she knew intuitively of his coming death a few months before it happened!

You will recall, as was mentioned on page 25 of this book, that on John's final visit home his sister felt something was not right.

The friends, as well as the family, remarked how exceptionally content and happy John was; there was no frustration or tension in his visit.

He laughed and talked easily with everyone, making it a point to visit all his old friends as well as the entire family.

He was no longer tense or worried about anything as was his usual, perfectionist make-up. [FACT: Depressed people often commit suicide when their symptoms seems to be improving.]

Everyone was happy, that is everyone except John's sister. His visit had left her with a sick panic that she could not even verbalize until a week after he had returned to his home.

It was then that she wakened in the early morning hours extremely distraught. Her husband found her quietly weeping at the kitchen table. Her explanation was simply that John was going to die by the first of the year unless someone could reach him. It was October.

[FACT: We do not experience any event of great depth in life without prior intuitive knowledge. This is more obviously manifested in a chart with a heavy Neptune influence.]

No amount of consolation relieved her and phone conversations with John did not bring anything to light. John insisted he was happy and content; everything was fine.

Her anxiety would not let up. The helplessness and futility was overwhelming; it was out of her control. Less than two months went by and John committed suicide. She lost him!

The shock was too much. RAGE* and confusion enveloped her; she rejected his death by withdrawing from life.

I explained to John's sister that before I began the chart comparison [Synastry] I would like to explain to her - first - her behavior reaction to the loss of love and - second - the planetary influences behind this behavior. Her outlook [Ascendant] played a big part in this behavior reaction.

DENIAL*

Psychology believes that when the shock is too great for an individual to accept - denial takes place.

Denial is a defense mechanism where a person suffering a psychosis [a mental disorder characterized by withdrawal] escapes the psychic pain or anxiety associated with reality by unconsciously rejecting reality.

This often happens as a result of a tragedy.

The year of the suicide Directed Neptune contacted the Sun/Neptune midpoint accentuating heightened sensitivity.

When Transiting Uranus activited her Natal Aquarian Sun and Mercury midpoints - Uranus/Neptune/Pluto - it ignited 'sudden development.'

Directed Saturn to the Ascendant brought despair as well as structure to this development.

PLANETARY KEYWORDS

URANUS........SUDDEN
NEPTUNE.......SENSITIVITY
PLUTO.........INTENSITY

SATURN........DEPRESSION/LOSS
ASCENDANT.....OUTLOOK/ENVIRONMENT

DEPRESSION*
Her time of anguish eventually became

a time of hope. She experienced Saturn depression and despair, but the energies of the planet were not wasted; from depression and despair emerged discipline and a new intellectual development.

ACCEPTANCE*

Directed Sun contacted the Mars/-Jupiter - creative birth - midpoint contact. It was the birth of a new love in her life; her new intellectual career. John came to her under birth aspects and he left her with a potential new 'birth' of intellect. Transiting Pluto to natal Jupiter had elevated her intellectually; her perception of life had been transformed.

This made possible the development of her Venus/Pluto love nature which was meant to enlarge to universal expression through intellectual development.

To return to the planetary beginning of the brother/sister relationship.

I explained the intense natal contacts of mothering that tied John to her; the manifestation of her ardent Pluto in the loving Cancer 5th house contacting her possessive, insecure Capricorn Venus.

This natal contact, along with the planetary directions and transits at the time he entered her life, strongly accentuated a sudden, emotional love need at last satisfied through mothering.

The year of his birth saw Directed Uranus contact her natal Venus indicating a sudden love in her life.

Directed Venus and Directed Ascendant contacted her natal Moon with the Mars/Jupiter/MC midpoints indicating 'a happy birth.'

Sun/Uranus-Pluto - midpoints in the Moon structure - indicate an individual transformation. Jupiter/Ascendant tells you something about the great happiness in the environment.

MOON [natal structure]

MARS........	....MC
MARS........	....JUPITER
JUPITER..	....ASCENDANT
SUN........	....URANUS/PLUTO

PLANETARY KEYWORD INTERPRETATION OF ABOVE MOON STRUCTURE ACTIVATED BY VENUS-ASCENDANT DIRECTIONS

Moon/Mars/MC
Energetic Mother [Moon/MC Female with

a purpose].

<u>Moon/Mars/Jupiter</u>
Happy Mother

<u>Moon/Jupiter/Ascendant</u>
Happy Emotional Environment

<u>Sun/Uranus/Pluto</u>
Individual [Sun] Change [Uranus/-Pluto] or Individual Transformation

The above Directions plus Transiting Jupiter to her natal Uranus/Ascendant midpoint told exactly how a little girl, just a matter of days before her 7th birthday, experienced a most precious period of her life. She became a mother!

John's sister spoke to the astrological birth explanation that I had made her aware of. "My father brought my mother home from the hospital and she permitted me to hold my new, little baby brother."

I can still recall the rush of possessive feeling that overwhelmed me as I held this tiny, helpless, sleeping baby in my arms.

Secretly, I knew he was not mother's

baby; he was mine! I would love and care for him better than anyone in the whole world would ever be able to."

She found in a male the emotional satisfaction her Natal Sun-Saturn had been seeking. This satisfaction had been rightfully denied by her much-loved, austere, duty-bound father through his exact Saturn contact to her emotional Moon.

An aspect that held back all the hugs and affection that emotionally dependant Pisces Ascendant and insecure Venus in Capricorn desperately needed for a sense of security from a male in her life.

"It was amazing," she continued, "John became so much more capable than I so quickly that emotional comfort was the only thing I felt I had to offer him."

She was beginning to discuss one of their most potent contacts between charts; their Venus/Saturn contact.

KEYWORDS:

VENUS......LOVE/CREATIVITY
SATURN.....SECURITY

I read her the textbook comment on the Venus/Saturn contact between charts:

Saturn stabilizes the emotions of Venus, feels great responsibility for Venus, expresses criticism and feeds on Venus affection. Saturn can be cold and distant. Venus gives constant love and reassurance; Venus in some way looks up to and reveres Saturn.

"This was quite true," she stated. "He made all my decisions and his criticism of my shortcomings was given in such a manner as to be praise; it was something that always gave me confidence.

For example, I would moan about how annoying my temperament was to me; I always wanted to be able to drive on the turnpikes to distant places, but I always became so nervous I would get lost.

He would say, quite annoyed and matter of factly, 'Why in heavens name do you worry about such mundane things when you are so God-awful talented!' And suddenly, I felt special and unique; with a single sentence he took away all my inadequate feelings, leaving me with such rational confidence in myself."

A good Saturn reassures, sometimes caustically; another textbook Venus/-Saturn sentence that incredibly pointed out the uniqueness of the contact.

In some cases where the Saturn individual does not have confidence in himself, then Saturn can be crushing to the Venus party. This, of course, was not the case in this relationship.

Astrologically the 3°-12" orb made the Venus/Saturn contact even more important. [ORB - space within which a planetary contact is judged to be effective].

The closer the orb with the Venus/-Saturn, the heavier would be the manifestation between the two charts.

The loyalty and love were so strong. I told her how she, the Venus party, must have boosted his morale in many ways and he, in his Saturn fashion protected her and gave her a feeling of safety.

This last explanation seemed to make her come alive; it was as if she now had the comfort she had been subconsciously searching for in seeking out this synastry explanation. She spoke excitedly about something that she had wondered about for years.

"When John died and his clothes and personal belongings were sent home there was a piece of paper in the coat pocket of one of his jackets.

It was a torn part of a letter I had written him. It praised his accomplishments, listing them, line by line, as if to make him more aware of his importance, ending with my great sense of love and pride in having a "baby brother" accomplish so much in such a short space of time."

The piece of paper was dogeared and worn and yet the jacket was new, something he had recently purchased before his death. The words had been supportive enough to have been in that pocket at the time of his death.

There had been more confusion than reassurance from that piece of paper until Astrology verified the desperate need for Saturn to hear of his accomplishments from the Venus loved one.

'To raise the confidence through consistent praise backed by love and affection' was actual textbook interpretation of the Venus/Saturn contact that had been read to her.

The office was suddenly quiet. She was deeply touched. Clinically, you could feel her Venus in Capricorn struggling to keep the Pisces Ascendant emotions under control. The verification that she had been necessary to John had created this rare moment of emotional comfort; a moment only synastry could have brought to her.

I began again with the two charts. I mentioned to her the other side of the Venus/Saturn coin. An ineffective Saturn can be extremely selfish with Venus, very intense and demanding of her time and attentions.

Her eyes held momentary rage for me. "I loved his selfishness," she stated emphatically as if to erase what she considered a clumsy transgression.

"I considered that trait very 'male' and something exceedingly lovable. I never wanted to change any part of him; I just always hoped to be a small part of his life."

She then recalled their extensive shopping trips on his visits home. "He would no sooner arrive than we would have to rush all over town shopping for the latest gimmick he had decided would make his life more interesting."

I mentioned his Mars contacted her Sun by close orb indicating he would out-energize her in all probability.

She backed this up instantly with the continuance of her shopping-trip story. She recalled one visit home that catapaulted into five, solid day and night shopping trips ending only at store closing times.

"That was the time he was pricing motor bikes to use on campus; it was the rage and all the professors were using them."

It took her almost a week to recupe from that visit. His Scorpio intensity, his strong Aries planets, his dogged Capricorn insistence and his Sagittarian always-on-the-go Moon were definitely too much energy for her passive earth and air chart with the water ascendant.

She was talking another important contact between their charts when she commented on his affectionate ways. You see his loving Venus contacting her self expressive Sun with this comment.

"He would always say, 'Now you just tell me when you get tired and we can go right home' or 'Are you sure you're not tired?' These were the little sentences, the intellectual affection, that kept me walking until I dropped.

There were many times when we had to stop and get a coke for that last lap. He would stand waiting patiently while I drank it, watching the liquid in the pop bottle slowly disappear; it was almost like re-fueling at a gas station. Then we were off again."
[A Saturn/Venus - Venus/Sun team]

"He once said, quite puzzled, 'You know, I'm amazed the way you love shopping with me that you don't shop like this when I'm out of town.'"

She had agreed with his amazement enthusiastically, secretly pleased he never knew she was exhausted and loathed shopping except with him. With John she was truly herself, a passive, self-sacrificing Pisces martyr and she loved every minute of it.

The Astrological consultation continued. His Venus contacted not only your Sun with a close orb of 1°27", but also made contact with your Mercury with an even closer orb of 0°21".

This contact indicated the dearest of comrades. There was sympathy, generosity, devotion, loyalty, love and easy communication between charts with these closely blended planetary contacts between charts.

She recounted in her conversations with John that often times at the end of the conversation she would say, "I love you sweetie" knowing she was demanding emotional reassurance. "He always gave it responding with, 'I love you too.'"

She had often felt guilty, aware of how stifling her emotionally dependent nature must have been for him; but, unable to stop the need from manifesting.

Astrologically,I begged to differ with her regarding her thinking that her emotions were stifling to him. His Venus contacting her Sun-Mercury and his Saturn contacting her Venus would say this emotional interchange was just what he needed.

His Venus with the Moon/Saturn midpoint indicated a lack of self confidence and a great sense of emotional loneliness.

He could not say it, but he needed very much to hear he was loved and appreciated.

Again, you could see through her sudden misty eyes the cold, protective Capricorn Venus control the quick, sensitive, Pisces-Neptune emotions.

She thanked me in business-like tones for the reassurance that her love had not been an oppressive burden for him, but a strong spiritual help benefiting both through their unique, brother-sister love bond.

She repeated once again that in no other consultation had she ever found so much concrete proof of the value of their relationship.

Her Synastry praise continued. The planetary confirmation conference, over all other therapeutic consultations, stood unique and alone in its excellence for giving her both emotional and intellectual comfort!

To return to John and his sister and their comparison contacts: His Mars on her Mercury and Sun indicated they must have had many energetic or lively [Mars] discussions.

Again, she agreed. We each had definite opinions and we each, at that time, came from different worlds. Hers narrow, bigoted and religious - his sophisticated, searching and, as yet, unstable and vulnerable.

His Pluto to her Jupiter gave her recognition and his Jupiter to her Uranus/Ascendant gave her sudden happiness through this recognition within the environment. Could she explain how this took place?

PLANETARY KEYWORDS:

PLUTO........RECOGNITION
JUPITER......HAPPINESS/EXPANSION
URANUS.......SUDDEN
ASCENDANT....OUTLOOK/ENVIRONMENT

SUMMARY: Recognition and Happiness Suddenly within the Environment.

She thought for a moment. Then she correlated the planetary keywords with the very definite explanation of how their energy manifested in her life.

"I was an artist. I studied with an internationally recognized oil painter and took many lessons at the local Art Institute as well as an Art Academy. [She spoke her Saturn = Sun/Venus midpoint manifesting as exacting art work].

When John came home from grad school to visit he would come to my apartment and scrupulously check over all my recently finished oils, water colors, and pastels hanging on the walls.

Then, he would take what he wanted for his apartment off the walls and stack them by the door. He was absolutely thrilled with his choices reminding me not to bang them around as I helped him carry them out to his car.

Then, he would call excitedly telling me of the comments made by different people that he entertained. Many were from New York and some of the larger cities and were quite experienced in the art field; their comments were most gratifying. I was forever thrilled to hear their praise through John."

This indeed was recognition. How subtly the planets manifest their energies!

Our consultation time had come to an end and it was satisfying to close with the lovely discussion of the happy-unique-recognition of the Jupiter/-Uranus/Pluto contact in her life.

We both looked forward to more planetary-discovery talks as she left with a lighter heart from our first

Astrological consultation.

SUMMARY OF SYNASTRY [CHART COMPARISON] CONTACTS BETWEEN JOHN AND HIS SISTER

JOHN	HIS SISTER

SATURN — VENUS

Saturn stabilizes the emotions of Venus, feels great responsibility for Venus, sometimes expresses criticism and feeds on Venus affection. Saturn can be cold and distant. Venus gives constant love and reassurance; Venus in some way looks up to and reveres Saturn.

MARS — SUN

Mars energizes and stimulates to action the Sun individual. This can be physically or a stimulation of the Sun individual's self expression.

VENUS — SUN

Harmony of love between Venus and the Sun. They are the dearest of comrades. There is sympathy, generosity, devotion,loyalty, love and easy communication between charts.

VENUS — MERCURY

Both benefit from intellectual discussion. There is intellectual understanding and mutual mental affection.

PLUTO JUPITER
Spiritual relationship. Mutual encouragement and inspiration.

JUPITER URANUS/ASCENDANT
Happiness and expansion develop the environment or enhance the outlook with new thinking.

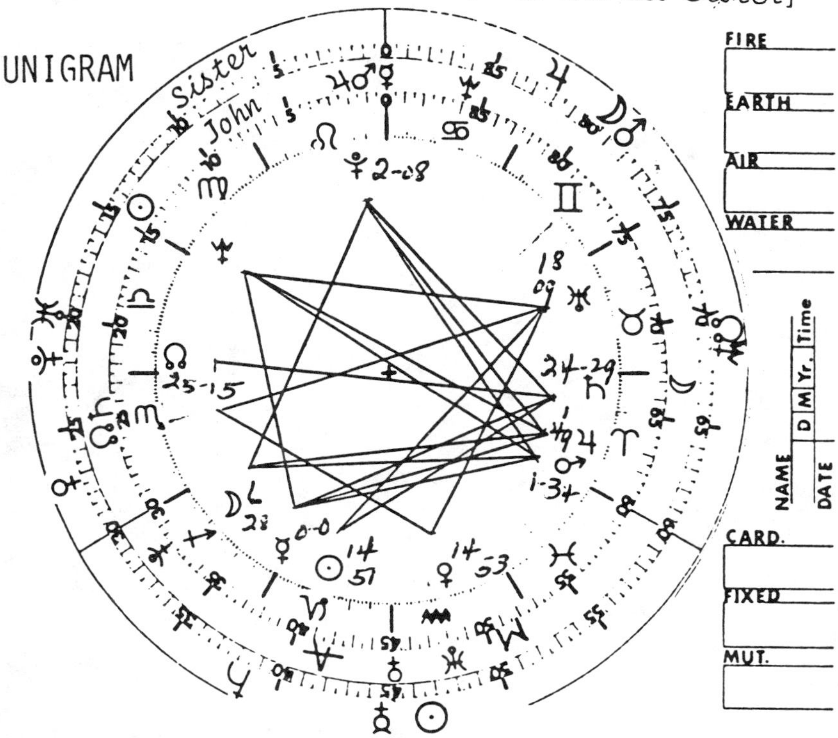

CONFIDENTIAL FILE #1
ILLUSTRATION #2
SYNASTRY [CHART COMPARISON]
JOHN AND HIS SISTER

JOHN'S NATAL CONFIGURATIONS

CARDINAL		
Mars in Aries	1 degree	34 minutes
Jupiter in Aries	1 degree	49 minutes
Saturn in Aries	24 degrees	29 minutes
Node in Libra	25 degrees	15 minutes
Sun in Capricorn	14 degrees	51 minutes
Mercury in Capricorn	0 degrees	0 minutes
FIXED		
Uranus in Taurus	18 degrees	09 minutes
Pluto in Leo	2 degrees	08 minutes
MC in Leo	20 degrees	35 minutes
Ascendant in Scorpio	11 degrees	36 minutes
Venus in Aquarius	14 degrees	53 minutes
MUTABLE		
Neptune in Virgo	25 degrees	29 minutes
Moon in Sagittarius	6 degrees	28 minutes

CHAPTER III

DISCOVER THE "LETHALITY" IN YOUR MARS ENERGY PATTERN!

Damned-up Mars energy flow without an outlet creates a combustible Mars condition. This is often the beginning of a lethal depression period that can ignite a suicide attempt!

Knowing how to guide and control your

vital Mars life force is not only necessary, but inescapable.

Necessary because understanding your Mars energy pattern is the only way you can make progress toward happy, successful living. Inescapable because without the knowledge of your Mars energy flow, life can become a circular pattern of unrest, frustration, inhibition or anger for you.

THE COMPLETE MARS ENERGY ANALYSIS CHART in this chapter will show you how to spot your energy blockages and, once recognized, how to correct the flow of energy so it becomes a benefit instead of a torment for you!

Not only will you find more understanding for yourself through this unique knowledge of your own Mars energy, but you will begin to recognize this flow of energy in others. This extraordinary new awareness will work to your advantage in creating better relationships for you!

As preparation for using THE COMPLETE MARS ENERGY ANALYSIS CHART, review the effective and ineffective keyword manifestations of Mars in different signs.

The following simplistic Mars energy

list is found in Karen's Keyword Compendium. The Compendium offers a unique keyword approach that provides complete natal, synastry and future interpretation. Right now, you are interested in a basic feel for the planet Mars in various signs.

MARS IN ARIES
COURAGEOUS OR BRUTAL

MARS IN TAURUS
POSSESSIVE OR STIFLING

MARS IN GEMINI
COMMUNICATIVE OR CUNNING

MARS IN CANCER
PROTECTIVE OR ABSORBING

MARS IN LEO
DOMINATING OR CRUEL

MARS IN VIRGO
ANALYTICAL OR CRITICAL

MARS IN LIBRA
CO-OPERATIVE OR OVERLY DEPENDENT

MARS IN SCORPIO
INTENSE OR RUTHLESS

MARS IN SAGITTARIUS
MOVING OR SCATTERED

MARS IN CAPRICORN
AMBITIOUS OR RUTHLESS

MARS IN AQUARIUS
INDEPENDENT OR REVOLUTIONARY

MARS IN PISCES
SELF SACRIFICING OR CONFUSED

Now that you have familiarized yourself with the very different 'extremes' of action of Mars in each sign you will want all the knowledge possible about your own unique natal Mars potential!

Make a complete discovery list of all your natal MARS contacts. You will use THE COMPLETE MARS ENERGY ANALYSIS CHART to interpret this list.

LISTING ALL YOU MARS ENERGY CONTACTS

[1.] Record all your natal aspects for Mars. This involves your 360° circle which is, of course, basic astrology.

[2.] Next, record your Mars midpoint

structure on this same piece of paper. This involves your 90° circle which is, of course, Ebertin's cosmobiology.

[3.] Lastly, record all "other midpoint structures" in your natal chart in which MARS appears. These structures also hold vital information for you as you will soon see in the exciting clarifying example from John's chart:

USE JOHN'S CHART AS A SAMPLE SHOWING YOU HOW TO LIST MARS ENERGY CONTACTS

1. PLANETARY LOCATION

Mars in Aries

2. PLANETARY ASPECTS [360° CIRCLE]

Mars trine Moon
Mars square Mercury
Mars semi-square Venus
Mars conjunct Jupiter
Mars parallel Jupiter
Mars semi-square Uranus
Mars opposition Neptune
Mars trine Pluto

3. MARS MIDPOINT STRUCTURE [90° CIRCLE]

MARS

MOON.....|.....SATURN

MOON.........	....NODE
MERCURY......	....MARS
MERCURY......	....JUPITER
VENUS........	....URANUS
VENUS........	....MC
MARS.........	....JUPITER
ASC..........	....MC

4. Very Important! LIST ALL OTHER MIDPOINT STRUCTURES WITH THE PLANET MARS APPEARING IN THE STRUCTURE FOR VALUABLE INFORMATION!

SUN = MARS/SATURN

SUN = MARS/NODE

MOON = MARS/ASCENDANT

MERCURY = MERCURY/MARS

MERCURY = MARS/NEPTUNE

VENUS = MERCURY/MARS

VENUS = MARS/NEPTUNE

JUPITER = MERCURY/MARS

JUPITER = MARS/JUPITER

SATURN = VENUS/MARS

SATURN = MARS/URANUS

URANUS = MARS/JUPITER

NODE = MARS/URANUS

NODE = MARS/MC

ASC = MARS/NEPTUNE

[UNIGRAM EXPLANATION IN GLOSSARY - Page 227]

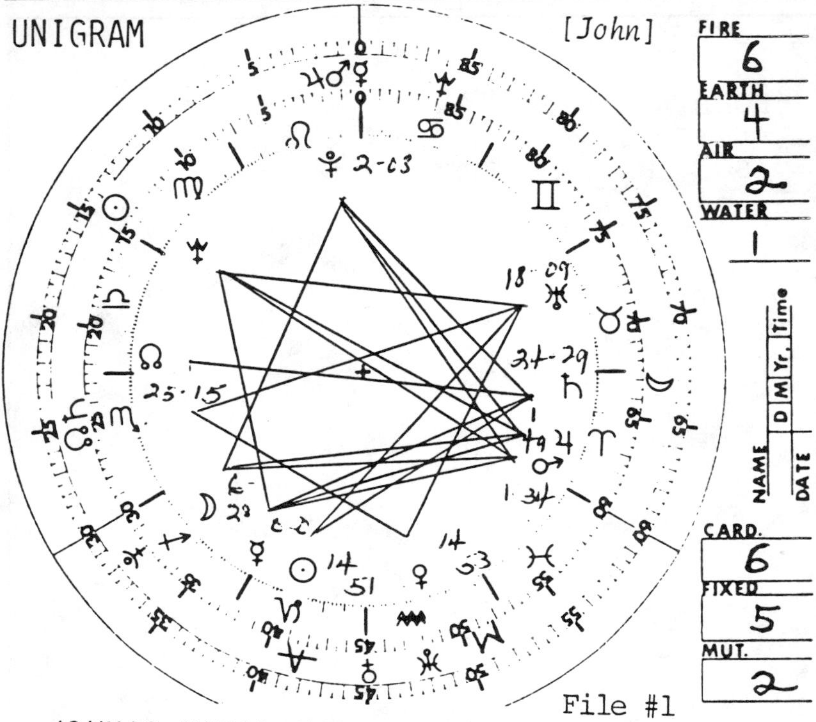

JOHN'S NATAL MARS CONTACTS

File #1
Illus.#3

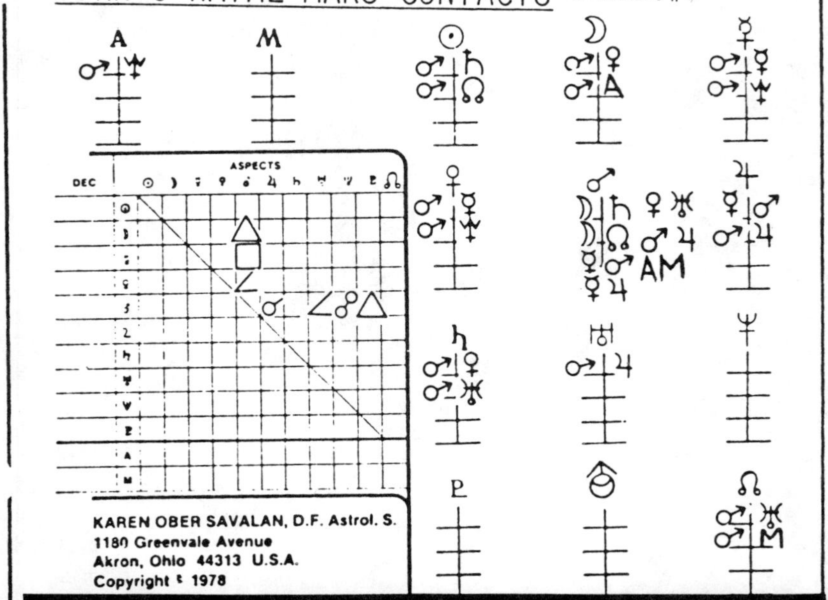

* UNIGRAM - See Glossary for fuller of Unigram form shown above.

NOW - for the exciting part!
Beside each group of Mars contacts, list just 'one' keyword for each planet. It is important that you use your favorite keyword: reason for this being your instinctive indentification with that energy and the way it influences you! For example, one person may think of Neptune in terms of 'confusion.' Another person will always see Neptune as 'spirituality.'

At a later time, you can play with other keywords with the very definite potential of a completely different interpretation for yourself. In the beginning, work closely with your one, familiar keyword.

This precise listing of your Mars contacts will reveal an energy-pattern that will astound you. You will make energy discoveries that you have never been aware of in yourself!

Once you discover the planets that influence your Mars energy the most, then you will use THE COMPLETE MARS ENERGY ANALYSIS CHART to manipulate these energies. You will see how you can magnetically draw great new benefits into your life as a result of knowing how to use these planetary energies.

This altered perception is going to

change your entire life.

SUMMARY

Up to this point you have learned how to list all your natal Mars contacts. Now you will discover how to interpret your MARS contacts.

HOW TO INTERPRET MARS ENERGY CONTACTS [USING JOHN'S CHART AS A SAMPLE]

[1.] Mars in Aries
Aggressive - Assertive - Courageous or Brutal

[2.]

MARS	ASPECTS - 360° CIRCLE
Mars/Moon	Energy Emotions
Mars/Mercury	Energy/Communication
Mars/Venus	Energy/Love
Mars/Jupiter	Energy/Opportunity
Mars/Uranus	Energy/Sudden
Mars/Neptune	Energy/Confusion
Mars/Pluto	Energy/Changes

In the section on aspects you will note what is LACKING. In other words, what planets do not make contact with Mars.

SUN and SATURN are missing! At this point, John is without a strong sense of self [SUN] or ability for discipline

[SATURN] that ties in with his energy [MARS]. You are very limited with interpretative information from the 360° circle only!

[3.] <u>MARS MIDPOINTS 90° CIRCLE</u>

MARS = MOON/SATURN
Energy/Emotions/Discipline

MARS = MOON/NODE
Energy/Emotions/Other People

MARS = MERCURY/MARS
Energy/Communication

MARS = MERCURY/JUPITER
Energy/Communication/Opportunities

MARS = VENUS/URANUS
Energy/Love/Sudden

MARS = MARS/JUPITER
Energy/Opportunities

MARS = ASCENDANT/MC
Energy/Environment/Ego

You now discover through midpoints some very definite correlations between energy, emotions, and discipline [MARS = MOON/SATURN]. This midpoint tells you that depression can come if the emotions are not kept reality oriented!

You see two locations with emphasis on

intellectual communication. They are MERCURY = MERCURY/MARS and MARS = MERCURY/JUPITER. Strong mental ability and energetic action of the mind for communication or argument are very evident.

MARS = VENUS/URANUS midpoint tells you that the energy [MARS] can be very passionate in its contact to VENUS and very sudden and romantic with its contacts to URANUS.

This is not enough information on the love picture. You want more. Where else in the chart can you go for more knowledge regarding the energy [Mars] and its interaction with love [Venus]?

The other midpoint structures hold more Mars discoveries! Check each structure starting with the Sun structure for Mars midpoints.

This will again change the overall interpretation by adding new strength and new weakness to many areas of the life.

The additional Mars structures can drastically change the total picture!

[4.] <u>ADDITIONAL MARS STRUCTURES</u>!

SUN = MARS/SATURN
Self/Energy/Discipline

SUN= MARS/NODE
Self/Energy/Other People

MOON = VENUS/MARS
Emotions/Love/Energy

MOON = MARS/ASCENDANT
Emotions/Energy/Environment

MERCURY = MERCURY/MARS
Communication/Energy

MERCURY = MARS/NEPTUNE
Communication/Energy/Confusion

VENUS = MERCURY/MARS
Love/Communication/Energy

VENUS = MARS/NEPTUNE
Love/Energy/Confusion

JUPITER = MERCURY/MARS
Opportunities/Communication/-
Energy

JUPITER = MARS/JUPITER
Opportunities/Energy

SATURN = VENUS/MARS
Discipline/Love/Energy

SATURN = MARS/URANUS
Discipline/Energy/Sudden

URANUS = MARS/JUPITER
Sudden/Energy/Opportunities

NODE = MARS/URANUS
Other people/Energy/Sudden

NODE = MARS/MC
Other people/Energy/Ego

ASCENDANT = MARS/NEPTUNE
Environment/Energy/Confusion

MORE discoveries! MOON = VENUS/MARS tells you that love involves strong, passionate feelings - nothing lukewarm about love feelings.

VENUS = MERCURY/MARS tells of much love discussion. VENUS = MARS/NEPTUNE can be either platonic or spiritual love relationships or confused, erotic unions.

The spiritual relationship was certainly the dear friend John lost through her suicide many years before his death.

SATURN = VENUS/MARS indicates the ability to discipline or place limits on a love relationship. Saturn ineffectively can also be illegitimate relationships. The energy-love picture is now complete.

In the section on Mars aspects we were disappointed to find Sun and Saturn absent from any contact with

Mars.

Midpoints change this. You now find good discipline and strength [Saturn] with the self [Sun] and the energy [Mars] through the Sun equals Mars/-Saturn midpoints. Self projection is now strongly secured!

Many structures emphasizing one planet make you aware of the big part that particular energy will play in the life of the individual.

For example, you see Neptune hiding in the structures in three places: MERCURY = MARS/NEPTUNE and VENUS = MARS/NEPTUNE and ASCENDANT = MARS/-NEPTUNE.

Since we have chose the keyword 'confusion' for Neptune in this chart, you will use this word in regard to the Neptune interpretation. You will then know Neptune has the ability to confuse the mind and communication through Mercury [MERCURY = MARS/-NEPTUNE] - the lovelife through Venus [VENUS = MARS/NEPTUNE] and the outlook and environment through the Ascendant [ASCENDANT = MARS/NEPTUNE].

In these three structure you have discovered the ideas of 'confusion' that can change this individual's whole life!

You see some very nice JUPITER opportunities present themselves through JUPITER = MERCURY/MARS and JUPITER = MARS/JUPITER. They can come suddenly through URANUS = MARS/JUPITER. The keyword 'opportunity' is frequent as will be the benefits in this chart. Becoming aware of this opportunity factor is half the battle toward pulling in the benefits!

Other people [Node] have a strong significance in John's chart in his life through SUN = MARS/NODE. Self expressive energy [MARS/NODE] combines with other people [NODE].

NODE = MARS/URANUS tells of sudden energy or quick decisions with others. Ego energy comes through the NODE = MARS/MC structure.

This gives you a surface idea of how to list and interpret your own natal Mars contacts.

Next, you will want answers as to how to use and manipulate planetary directions and transits for yourself to get the full benefits from your Mars contacts.

These easy-to-follow, unique planetary

answers for coping with planetary stress can all be found in THE COMPLETE MARS ENERGY ANALYSIS CHART. It is your guide to planetary happiness and opportunity.

THE COMPLETE MARS ENERGY ANALYSIS CHART is divided into three, very easy, unique sections. They are:

[1.] Red light behavior
Blocked Mars energy

Here you learn how to easily spot Mars energy blockages in yourself as well as in those around you through observation of potent Mars behavior!

[2.] Underlying Mars energy dynamics

In this section you will discover the cause of the physical forces behind the Mars behavior reactions!

[3.] Mars Rescue Combating Method

This will be your solution. It will not be easy, but it promises a guaranteed reward. If you follow the suggested 'control pattern' you will arrive at eventual success.

MARS ENERGY ANALYSIS CHART

MARS/SUN

[1.] Red light MARS/SUN behavior!
Blocked energy!

The Mars/Sun person is aggressively

hostile, stubborn and obstinate when the energy is blocked. Belligerant behavior is much in evidence. The Mars/Sun person will be continually fighting something; always in active opposition, struggling to resist with or against another person or object.

You experience constant risk taking, quarreling, contradiction or actual physical unrest with this person. The fighting behavior can go so far as actually kicking things, breaking things, throwing things; in general demanding attention through force!

[2.] Underlying MARS/SUN energy dynamics!

The planet Mars, being true to its catalytic nature, constantly pushes, energizes, activates and literally agitates the Sun individual for some action of self expression.

The Sun person is forced to cope with this disturbing, churning, demanding aggressive energy to maintain inner peace. The self expression or individuality of the Sun person is forced to find an outlet or release for this upsetting, fighting energy.

NOTE: MARS/SUN energy can manifest as strong energy or brutal energy from a 'male' to you or from you to a 'male'!

[3.] Rescue Combating Method for MARS/SUN

Competition must come into play. It is useless for the Mars/Sun energy person to run from this 'fighting energy' because Mars will continue to maintain its volatile fighting principle attacking the Sun self expression for action.

The Sun person is forced to cope with this disturbing, churning, demanding aggressive Mars energy to maintain inner peace.

Release occurs only through competition or trying for the lead in some area of life. The Mars/Sun person may 'compete' with a person, a thing or an idea but this energy must find its way home through a striving to outdo another for supremacy in some way.

Physical competition as well as mental competition is the Rescue Combating Method for Mars/Sun.

MARS/MOON

[1.] Red light MARS/MOON Behavior! Blocked energy!

Blocked energy makes the Mars/Moon person intolerant, impulsive, hot tempered, unpredictable and instantly upset.

There will be violent emotional outbreaks, hysteria, fits of uncontrollable laughter or weeping and an extreme intolerance or rebellion of one's feelings.

The behavior goes to extreme stages of excessive excitement; the individual exhibiting uncontrollable outbursts of emotion over a very insignificant factor.

[2.] Underlying MARS/MOON energy dynamics

Mars so forcefully energizes the Moon emotions that it causes them to become 'fighting emotions.' The highly charged feelings can never be lukewarm about anything. There is either great enthusiasm and excitability or complete disinterest about even the most mundane things.

Hot feelings, fits of passion and much temperament come into play when violent, catalytic Mars energy goads gentle, sensitive Moon emotion into constant, hasty, unreasonable emotionalism. To be rational many times takes that moment longer than the Moon emotions can handle after a fiery Mars contact!

NOTE: MARS/MOON energy can manifest as strong energy or brutal energy from a female, the family or the public to you or vice versa from you to a female, the family or the public. [Female, family and the public are, of course, all represented by the Moon].

[3.] Rescue Combating Method for MARS/MOON

Since it is impossible to take the rebel out of the naturally rebellious Mars/Moon contact you must give the rebel an outlet for that energy - "a cause."

This "cause" can be a person or a thing that produces a result, an ideal or a goal to which the aggressive, volatile Mars/Moon can become dedicated.

Daily the bulk of energy must be channelled into work of some constructive nature for this "cause" as an outlet for the fiery emotional nature. It can then exhibit its strong feelings of pleasure, pain, grief, joy, etc. for this "cause."

The Moon represents the family; thus Mars/Moon energy can accomplish great things for the individual family members. The Moon also represents the public. Here Mars/Moon can use its strong, excitable energetic drive in a public-oriented goal or business.

Find a "cause" to become dedicated to for your agitated Mars/Moon personality and you have the solution for their blocked energies!

MARS/MERCURY

[1.] Red light MARS/MERCURY Behavior! Blocked energy

The Mars/Mercury person operating under blocked energy will shock you by spewing forth violent, caustic verbal abuse without due cause. Speech will be quarrelsome in the extreme.

The individual will be a constant fault finder. Ineffectively the Mars/-Mercury energy will manifest as a very prejudiced, obstinate individual. He will be touchy, snappish, cranky, and impatient. Bitter quarrels will be common with this type of person. To summarize - others will view the individual as a bitter, provocative malcontent.

[2.] Underlying MARS/MERCURY energy

dynamics

The force of Mars activates the thinking with such great energy that the individual can't keep a tranquil state of mind. This strong mental energy must have an outlet of expression where it can free itself of this mental-energy build-up.

Mars energy constantly hammers the Mercury mind with catalytic force. Verbal explosions result from the churning of this mental energy. A type of mental combustion is the result.

Others cannot understand the high nervous tension the Mars/Mercury person is under. Therefore, the Mars/Mercury person will suffer from two areas: mental pressure and misunderstanding of his high nervous tension by others. At times a nervous breakdown can occur.

NOTE: MARS/MERCURY energy can manifest as forceful communication or brutal communication from a 'male' to you or from you to a 'male.'

[3.] Rescue Combating Method for MARS/MERCURY

The mind must have training, education, and instruction. It must be exposed to books, the arts, science or to any subject for the purpose of learning.

The individual will benefit enormously through a sincere diligence at any branch of learning undertaken for mental improvement.

The mind can then exhibit its powerful strength and vigor in an effective manner. Its untiring capabilities can excel in structured areas of communication that deal in writing, reporting, debating, public speaking or occupations and hobbies that have to do with a communicative background.

Creating an outlet through training, education or instruction for the strained Mars/Mercury mental energy will automatically result in the improvement of the health.

MARS/VENUS

[1.] Red light MARS/VENUS Behavior
Blocked energy!

The seductive, passionate behavior of the carefree playboy or playgirl is nothing more than ineffective, blocked Mars/Venus energy.

Sexual overtones or unbridled passionate advances that go with the pleasure seeker are evidences of the troubled Mars/Venus behavior.

Sensuous remarks, always with a prelude to a sexual conquest or remarks with an emphasis on sexual coquettery are indicative of a surplus of love energy with no structure developed to provide an outlet other than seeking a sexual partner.

[2.] Underlying MARS/VENUS energy dynamics

Mars energy, excessively aggressive by nature, contacts Venus love/creative make-up and emotionally energizes it. The result is an extremely lustful person or an extremely devotional, creative or spiritual person.

There is not much leeway for cooperation or compromise with a Mars/Venus individual. Mars brings energetic stimulation to Venus and the result inevitably will be energetic love or energetic creativity - at what level depending upon what Venus can bring to the contact.

There is no pacifier except forceful creative love action of some kind! Venus love can go either way as stated above; powerfully spiritual and inspirational or powerfully sensual and sexual.

NOTE: MARS/VENUS energy can manifest as harmonious passion or disharmonious passion in a relationship.

[3.] Rescue Combating Method for MARS/VENUS

There is enormous talent for creativity in the Mars/Venus contact, but willpower and discipline are necessary to refine the energy for this creative potential.

The Mars/Venus energetic love can become refined through training in the development of skills and techniques in creative pursuits. This can include happiness through creative ventures in art, music, entertainment, or through socializing.

Socializing that would bring Mars/Venus the most peace and harmony would come through social groups specializing in creative action with definite goals and purposes.

Refined love or structured love to many can become outstanding when Mars/Venus becomes the polished, elegant creative force in a social group with humanitarian aims.

Lastly, on a personal level, Mars/-Venus will find inner contentment if the love energy is manifested as devotional love to one person rather than an emphasis on many physical love contacts lacking true Mars/Venus balance.

MARS/JUPITER

[1.] Red light MARS/JUPITER behavior! Blocked energy

Exaggerated rebelliousness will show itself in many ways when Mars blocks the Jupiter philosophic, cooperative principle and creates ineffective behavior.

There is definite refusal to obey or to revolt from people to which there has been an allegiance.

Over-strained behavior in work or play is the keynote. Pride, arrogance, rash action, avarice and in general an attitude of "too much" is exhibited in the person's behavior. The Jupiter generosity, giving principle then becomes ineffectively energized Mars/Jupiter energy.

There can be "too much" drinking - "too much" socializing - "too much" eating - "too much" spending and on and on. In short, an obvious lack of moderation in behavior along with a rebellious note is in evidence when Mars/Jupiter energy is in trouble!

[2.] <u>Underlying MARS/JUPITER energy dynamics</u>

Over energizing and over enthusiasm is the result of Mars coming into contact with Jupiter.

Mars supplies its usual amount of forceful catalytic energy to benefit Jupiter for its use. The result of this Mars/Jupiter combination is always an overabundance of energy as Jupiter's giving principle, being heavily energized, becomes extravagant with the forceful Mars energy.

For any effective results, Jupiter is forced to draw hard lines. This is as difficult for kind, gentle Jupiter as it is for compassionate, forgiving Neptune.

Keeping the extravagant energy in check will always take discipline.

Picture a balloon - if you forcefully

blow air into it, it gets bigger and bigger. Eventually, it will bust unless you use the Rescue combating method for Mars/Jupiter in the next paragraph to keep your balloon intact!

NOTE: MARS/JUPITER energy can manifest as enthusiastic energy or extravagant energy from a 'male' to you or from you to a 'male!'

[3.] Rescue combating method for MARS/JUPITER

When energies expand at a rapid rate, there must be a control to handle the inevitable reckless results.

The high energy level and the strong forceful enthusiasms resulting from the Mars/Jupiter combination will always run rampant with enthusiasm; so they must be able to perform functions that suit their rampant-running styles.

Using the natural 'promotional' thrust of the contact is the answer to the problem. Mars/Jupiter energy naturally excites, encourages, enlarges, increases and advances. These enthusiastic promotional energies need a 'constructive element' behind the highly-spirited thrust.

A constructive element involves structure which gives the ability to build, devise, put together, arrange and form. Combine a constructive element with promotion in any area and you rescue Mars/Jupiter from dissipating its energy.

Now you have high enthusiasms and practical action - an unbeatable combination. The balloon that fills 'slowly' and expands easily and with safety. Result: many well proportioned balloons instead of a succession of huge, recklessly expanded bursted balloons!

MARS/SATURN

[1.] Red light MARS/SATURN behavior! Blocked energy

Extreme impatience, sullen anger, consistent negative attitudes, and cruelty are all manifestations of blocked Mars/Saturn energy.

The predominate signal of the ineffective manifestation is that the energies have no moderation; they run either hot or cold and are always furious or depressed.

Cruelty is another sign of blocked Mars/Saturn energy. The individual is not only hard-hearted, but actually seems to enjoy causing upsets, distress, pain or grief to another person. This tormenting type of energy can manifest through verbal, emotional or physical abuse.

Possibly <u>ineffective</u> Mars/Saturn behavior could react as follows with the different signs:

<u>ARIES</u> Mars/Saturn could easily be physical abuse.

<u>TAURUS</u> Mars/Saturn could frustrate others with a determination and a persistence toward hanging on to outmoded thinking.

<u>GEMINI</u> Mars/Saturn could exhibit cruelty, of a very skillful nature, undermining relationships in a very insidious way.

<u>CANCER</u> Mars/Saturn could be tops at exhibiting 'manipulative' cruelty with others, pitting one family member or friend against another, exercising a very subtle, type of oppressive control over their lives.

<u>LEO</u> Mars/Saturn could be the domineering, cruel tyrant relentlessly interfering with everyone's life.

<u>VIRGO</u> Mars/Saturn could exhibit a caustic, cruel mental energy that could be very life-denying to those with

whom the Virgo contacts on a consistent basis.

LIBRA and PISCES Mars/Saturn could easily permit the Mars/Saturn cruelty to go inward toward escapism of some type; alcohol, drugs, sex, etc.

SCORPIO Mars/Saturn could be an actual threat to anyone in conflict with him because of the vindictivenss of the nature.

CAPRICORN Mars/Saturn would show a very definite cunning or treacherous type of emotional cruelty because in-effective Capricorn loves to play games with people's lives.

And lastly, AQUARIUS Mars/Saturn would exhibit its cruelty in a rebellious way; going against a cause or society itself.

[2.] Underlying MARS/SATURN energy dynamics

Mars is your drive; your energy action that moves you forward in life.
Saturn is reality, a force that permits no imagination or pretense; a selfless, enduring, moderation principle.

Imagine these two energies; one young, eager, impetuous and another old, wise, moderate and accepting working together on a project. What will occur?

Tension and frustration, of course.

To fully understand the "frustration-from-conflict" dynamics of Mars/-Saturn energy, read the following story of changing keywords in the Mars/Saturn/Neptune tale.

NOTE: MARS/SATURN energy can manifest as disciplined energy or cruel energy from a 'male' to you or from you to a 'male.'

DRAMATIC 'MARS/SATURN/NEPTUNE' TALE OF CHANGING KEYWORDS!

Mars/Neptune meets a difficult problem in life; refuses Saturn discipline and turns to escapism. Mars/Neptune starts to drink. Keywords read:

MARS/NEPTUNE	Escapist Energy
SATURN	Discipline

Saturn tries to bring reality through frustration. Mars/Neptune's drinking brings impotence. Keywords are changing:

MARS/NEPTUNE	Impotence
SATURN	Frustration

Mars/Neptune refuses reality; the drinking problem continues. Life becomes hell at home, at work - everywhere. Saturn continues to bring reality. Keywords are now:

MARS/NEPTUNE	Confusion/Chaos
SATURN	Reality

Lying, hiding liquor, running becomes a way of life. Saturn endures, continues to teach. Keywords change again:

MARS/NEPTUNE	Cunning and Treachery
SATURN	Endurance

A fall down the cellar stairs - a fall in the bathtub - a serious car accident on the way to the store. Saturn continues to teach. Keywords become:

MARS/NEPTUNE	Accidents/Tragedy
SATURN	Reality - Brush with death

Mars/Neptune is hospitalized. Saturn comes to the rescue for Mars/Neptune.

Saturn is there with a recovery program for chemical abuse as well as with a volunteer from Alcoholics Anonymous. Keywords become effective:

MARS/NEPTUNE	Intellectual Energy
SATURN	Stability

Mars/Neptune sees life through Saturn's eyes. Reality is good! Mars/Neptune becomes an active, well-loved and appreciated member of Alcoholics Anonymous. The lesson has been learned. Keywords become elevated:

MARS/NEPTUNE	Spiritual Energy
SATURN	The Teacher

An interesting keyword story has just explained uniquely the energy dynamics of Mars/Saturn with another planet!

[3.] Rescue Combating Method for MARS/SATURN

Conflict and frustration must be rationally approached and resolved. Conflict is the battle or struggle to resolve the demands of the eager, impulsive Mars energy and the restricting, structured Saturn energy working together. Frustration results from constantly working with two opposites.

Acceptance will come from an intellectual view of the workings of the energies. A certain area of the work will bring 'no satisfaction'. This does not mean 'no progress' or 'no success'; it merely means unfulfilled emotional satisfaction in the action of the work.

A longer view of the work spells progress and success. To be able to see a prosperous, fortunate future as a result of frustrated work can be something lesser energetic charts dare but dream of.

Frustration and tension therefore must be seen as 'energizers' and enviable tools toward success! The long view is the answer for combating Mars/Saturn.

[1.] Red light MARS/URANUS behavior! <u>Blocked energy</u>

Bluntness, hot temper, excitability and nervous tension are natural responses by all of us on occasion.

When this ineffective behavior becomes consistent and the individual is not concerned with the consequences of the erratic pattern then you know you are dealing with blocked energy in a reckless Mars/Uranus individual.

The Mars/Uranus person exhibits no patience or diplomacy. He is headstrong and generally a risk taker.

Self will and lack of co-operation keep the individual from fitting in with others. His actions are fitful and irritable.

A good part of the time he operates under tension headaches from this chaotic rhythm. Noise - disturbance - disorder and confusion are always in evidence when the Mars/Uranus energy is blocked.

Summary: Blocked Mars/Uranus energy manifests as a peculiar, erratic type of energy having no definite course of action.

This erratic behavior includes doing consistently crazy things that momentarily catch the Mars/Uranus individual's interest. The Mars/Uranus individual does not consider the outcome of his upsetting, disturbing actions upon others.

[2.] Underlying MARS/URANUS energy dynamics

See the change that is created as a

result of the combination of Mars energy and Uranus energy. KEYWORDS tell this enlightening story very easily and clearly!

MARS KEYWORDS	URANUS KEYWORDS
ENERGY	AWAKENER
ACTION	SUDDEN
FORCE	DEVELOPMENT
DRIVE	STRONG WILLED
CATALYST	INDIVIDUALIST
VIGOR	GENIUS

MARS/URANUS KEYWORD COMBINED ACTION!

AWAKENED ENERGY!
SUDDEN ACTION!
DEVELOPMENT OF FORCE!
STRONG-WILLED DRIVE!
INDIVIDUALISTIC CATALYST!
VIGOROUS GENIUS!

WHAT HAVE YOU JUST SEEN?

In all of the Mars Uranus keyword combinations you've experienced the 'quickness' or the 'sudden energizing' without provocation or reason that takes place. Hence you are working with a force that must have a foundation established in order to handle this sudden action!

NOTE: MARS/URANUS energy can manifest as forceful energy or explosive energy from you to a 'male' or from a 'male' to you.

[3.] Rescue Combating Method for MARS/URANUS

You have just read about the Mars/Uranus combination of energies that creates a very unique force. Since the energies are so tremendously original and so active and ambitious you must create a channel for this unique originality. There must be an area in life that holds a stable, acceptable 'excitement'.

Life is at times dull, repetitious in its pattern and tedious. A condition of boredom is not easy for a Mars/Uranus person to tolerate therefore there must be an avenue of expression that eliminates this state of mental monotony.

A mental outlet is necessary to give the Mars/Uranus rapid, decisive willpower an opportunity to act in its sudden, original way. Structure keeps the energy from becoming eccentric.

The large amount of nervous energy can be fed through the original mental resources where they will not undermine the physical energies.

The sudden rejecting of old conditions and the creation of new concepts can then take place in the mental sphere of work where a sudden Mars/Uranus manifestation can be most effective. In short structure will lay groundwork for the potential Uranus genius and Mars energy combination to manifest.

[1.] Red Light MARS/NEPTUNE behavior! Blocked energy!

The Mars/Neptune person is in a state of great emotional confusion, many times bordering on emotional chaos when the energy is blocked.

Excited feelings such as screaming, crying, yelling, name-calling are all in evidence. Unreasonableness is the keynote.

The confusion and disorder from this high emotionalism makes it difficult to analyze the situation. Behavior is extremely fitful and outrageous; sometimes the person threatens great injury or wrong doing exceeding all bonds of reasonableness. The individual can be very offensive or shocking; the actions and disposition can be violent.

[2.] Underlying MARS/NEPTUNE energy dynamics!

Mars represents energy and Neptune represents imagination; consequently the combination of these two forces will generate great creative energy that demands an outlet.

The principles of energy and imagination or analysis and sensitivity will always come into play when these two planets are in contact with each other. It can be easily understood how Neptune sensitivity and imagination in contact with the Mars energy can make the person - if he is not disciplined - incapable of clear, organized thinking and acting!

Examining these two planetary energies through the simplistic keyword style makes you aware of their opposing natures. For example:

MARS KEYWORDS	NEPTUNE KEYWORDS
ENERGY	VAGUE
SEX DRIVE	ENTHUSIASTIC
ACTION	INSPIRATIONAL

AMBITION DISAPPOINTING

From the six keyword combinations you see the need for structure.

Vague energy demands clarity. Enthusiastic sex drive demands discrimination. Inspirational action requires limits. Disappointing ambition demands endurance. You understand the dynamics, now for the solution or rescue combating method for Mars/Neptune.

<u>NOTE:</u> MARS/NEPTUNE energy can manifest as inspirational energy or confused energy from a 'male' to you or from you to a 'male'.

[3.] Rescue Combating Method for MARS/NEPTUNE
<u>Train the 'imaginative' energy</u>

Mars/Neptune people must use the imaginative energy to dream, hope and anticipate life in some responsible way or the 'imagination' can create a fear-ridden, emotionally-tormented individual.

The heightened sensitivity that comes through the combination of Mars with Neptune generates a touchy, easily-offended, flight-oriented individual.

Mars/Neptune has great analytical power hidden within its structure. The mental energies are not only enormous [Neptune without limits and Mars energy] but they can be lofty and humanistic.

Mars/Neptune needs structure and routine more than any other planetary combination. This combination cries out for a strong Saturn to bring the discipline needed for the great imagination that lies behind this contact.

Mars/Neptune can benefit greatly from routine, organization, and moderation in eating, sleeping, playing or working habits.

Creative energy can take place beautifully when method and order combine with talent or creativity. Painting, writing, dancing, and listening to music are just a few of the creative areas which Mars/Neptune has available for training the imaginative talent.

[1.] Red light Mars/Pluto behavior
<u>Blocked energy</u>

The Mars/Pluto person by nature is extremely proud. When the energy is blocked the individual exalts his own importance and becomes arrogant and overbearing with others. The behavior manifests simply as an unreasonable conceit of one's own superiority over others.

The extremes resulting from this arrogance create a very dominating, ruthless individual who makes inordinate claims and demands upon others.

The negative Mars/Pluto person will be extremely manipulative using everyone to further his own life. He can be a demanding fanatic; reckless and extravagant in opinion and behavior.

When the Mars/Pluto energy is blocked the individual demands being catered to. He will be extremely vindictive if everything does not go his way.

Ineffectively the Mars/Pluto person can be merciless or pitiless in a relationship. He will go past the point of good taste in everything.

[2.] Underlying MARS/PLUTO energy dynamics

Pluto's basic thrust is transformation or change. It upsets status quo and changes conditions. Pluto brings an enormous amount of intense, dynamic energy to a planet and inevitably changes conditions by intensifying the forces of the planet it contacts.

When Pluto contacts Mars you have 'intense change' [Pluto] contacting 'energy' [Mars]. The result will be a transformation of the Mars energy through Pluto's extreme energizing.

Keywords help you to understand the action occurring when these two planetary forces make contact.

MARS	PLUTO
ENERGY	INTENSITY
AMBITION	FANATICISM
VIOLENCE	UPHEAVALS
CATALYTIC	TRANSFORMATIONS

Combine any of the above keywords and you immediately see the underlying energy dynamics. Energy is intensified! Ambition is fanaticized! Violence causes upheavals! Changes are ignited. Pluto's thrust is so potent that there must be a channel for this transformation to effectively take place.

[3.] Rescue Combating Method for MARS/PLUTO

Mars/Pluto demands a progressive outlet. There must be a step-by-step way in which this intense energy can move forward; a way to grow and increase that is effective.

To advance toward something better or moving toward a specific goal is the most beneficial manifestation of Mars/Pluto energy. The energy, courage and willpower that is generated from the coming together of these two forces must continually regenerate or change in a way that develops the individual's awareness.

This dynamic duo [Mars and Pluto] can use their 'ruthless fighting energy' for the advancement of progressive change. The stamina along with the transformation potential is so strong that it operates most effectively when there is a step-by-step plan toward some progressive goal.

Using the same combination of keywords listed under [2.] Underlying MARS/PLUTO energy dynamics you can see how the energies can be rescued.

Intense energy working in a step-by-step progressive outlet spells success. Fanatic ambition with guidelines will make suitable changes in its quest toward success. Even violent upheavals can ultimately spell advancement if the two forces can work through the transformation.

SUMMARY: What you have discovered in the previous chapter on MARS energy!

PLANETARY ENERGIES	UNIQUE SOLUTIONS FOR USING PLANETARY ENERGIES FOR THE MOST BENEFIT AND HAPPINESS
MARS/SUN	COMPETITION brings benefits and happiness to Mars/Sun.
MARS/MOON	Working at a DEDICATED CAUSE brings benefits and happiness to Mars/Moon.
MARS/MERCURY	MENTAL TRAINING brings benefits and happiness to Mars/Mercury.
MARS/VENUS	REFINED LOVE brings benefits and happiness to Mars/Venus.
MARS/JUPITER	CONSTRUCTIVE PROMOTIONAL activity brings benefits and happiness to Mars/Jupiter.
MARS/SATURN	THE LONG VIEW brings benefits and happiness to Mars/Saturn
MARS/URANUS	ORIGINAL MENTAL OUTLET brings benefits and

happiness to Mars/Uranus.

MARS/NEPTUNE	TRAINING THE IMAGINATIVE FACULTY brings benefits and happiness to Mars/Neptune.
MARS/PLUTO	PROGRESSIVE STEP-BY-STEP TRANSFORMATIONS bring benefits and happiness to Mars/Pluto.

Your Ascendant [Outlook and Environment] - your MC [Ego and Life Goals] and your Node [Contacts and Acquaintances] will be interpreted using the nine Mars energies explained in this chapter.

EXAMPLE:

ASCENDANT

MARS......NEPTUNE
MARS......PLUTO

Read for Mars/Neptune and apply the creative principle to your outlook or your environment. Then read for Mars/Pluto and apply the intensity to your outlook and your environment.

You have potential undermining [Mars/Neptune] in the environment and also potential domination [Mars/Pluto].

Effectively you can make this a creative environment [Mars/Neptune] with good work intensity [Mars/Pluto] used to offset the negative manifestation.

The author has purposely chosen not to give a stereotyped interpretation for Mars with the Ascendant, the MC or the Node. This is a personal area in which the reader must weigh the contacts from his own viewpoint to correctly guage the influence of the various Mars contacts to his Ascendant, MC and Node.

CHAPTER IV

ARE YOU A PLANETARY VICTIM?

The choice is yours!

Behavior is a result of the way a person reacts to planetary directions and transits.

An assertive person is one who supports

and maintains effective behavior or what he or she feels or has been taught is effective behavior. Unfortunately many times what one 'has been taught' or conditioned to believe is effective behavior is actually a very destructive mode of action!

There are enlightening planetary differences between types of behavior - effective and ineffective - that make you a victim or a victimizer. Ineffective behavior is recognized in a shockingly clear picture through confidential files showing reactions to life conditions that create actual suicide attempts!

To become a victim is to become sacrificed, injured, cheated or destroyed by another. To 'victimize' is of course the opposite - to sacrifice, injure, cheat or destroy another. When you react negatively to planetary transits and directions your energy automatically manifests as either a victim or a victimizer and you become the loser!

Being a 'victim' or a 'victimizer' are both negative behavior manifestations. The desired condition or what positive reactions to planetary transits and directions create is 'non-victim' behavior.

What is non-victim behavior? Non-victim planetary behavior is a way of acting that exhibits acceptable or efficient 'assertiveness'.

For example Mars energy is assertive, supportive and catalytic when it is manifesting effectively to planetary magnetism. When lines are not drawn Mars energy ineffectively becomes brutal, cruel or even accident prone; it then becomes the victim or the victimizer.

Jupiter in your chart can be eloquent in its philosophic behavior when you react effectively to its planetary rays. Jupiter can then be just the right amount of justice, wisdom or moderation for operation at peak level.

When you permit Jupiter energy to become ineffective and lose moderation you victimize yourself through extravagance. You become the Jupiter that buys his friends so he will have someone to pander to his ego. This behavior inevitably debilitates you both emotionally and financially.

Saturn can be efficiency, practicality, or discipline for you when operating effectively. On the other hand when you permit Saturn's energies to become inhibiting and depressive through lack of structure you become ineffective and unassertive. You can then become the martyr-type victim feeding off the emotional pity of others.

Saturn can also victimize by placing too much emphasis on duty either for himself or for those around him (the victims). This behavior can be extremely cruel and oppressive.

The role of victim and victimizer in the manifestation of Uranus energy is obvious! Instead of becoming strong-willed and resourceful, Uranus will victimize through a disruptive, stubborn, arrogant, non-co-operative manner or permit another to victimize him in this manner.

Neptune's kindness and compassion when operating effectively is like witnessing a miracle of love. When Neptune refuses to draw lines you see chaotic confusion. This confusion creates the ineffectual 'doormat' who is victimized.

Effectively Pluto's intense nature can help judge and direct weaker souls. Ineffectively Pluto can tyrannically victimize and destroy all within its range through its extreme domination or vindictiveness.

Following are everyday planetary life situations that possess a uniqueness in the casting of the role of 'victim' or 'victimizer'. You will inevitably find yourself in some of the planetary life conditions creating the victim/victimizer syndrome. Personal circumstances naturally will be different but if you look closely at the 'life condition' created you will recognize a time when you were either a victim or the victimizer!

QUESTION: Why investigate confidential files showing everyday planetary life situations demonstrating victim/victimizer roles?

ANSWER: Because some people caste in the roles of victim/victimizer find these roles so intolerable, so life-denying and so inescapable that they attempt suicide! The following 'attempters' were those people.

For the sake of discretion the names of the confidential case studies have been changed.

NETTIE

AN ATTEMPTER!

FAMILY VICTIMIZATION!

UNIGRAM

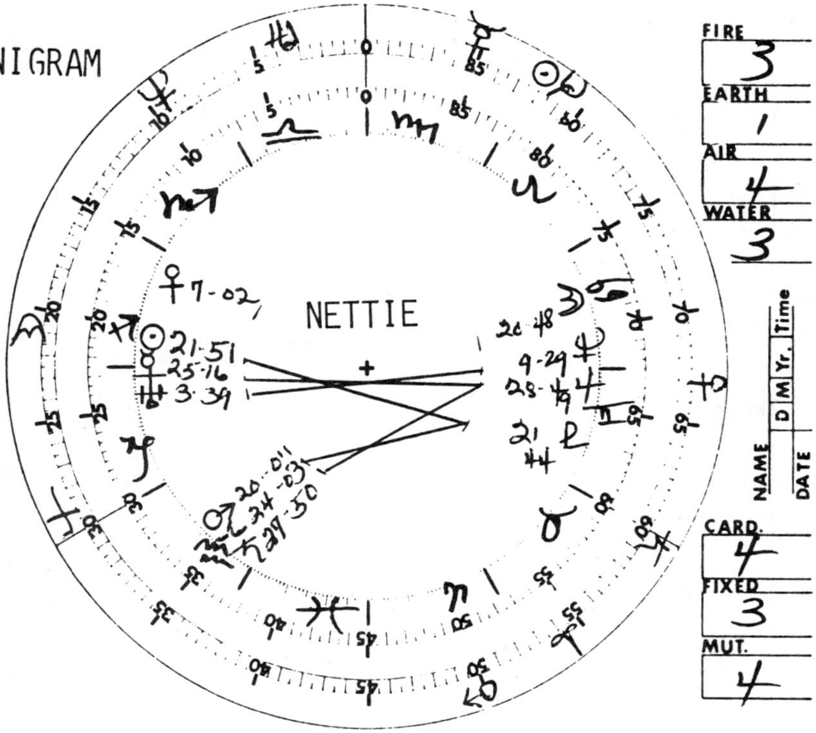

CONFIDENTIAL FILE # 2
ILLUSTRATION # 4
"A WILLING FAMILY VICTIM"
FEMALE - NETTIE

CARDINAL		
Neptune in Cancer	9 degrees	29 minutes
Moon in Cancer	20 degrees	48 minutes
Jupiter in Cancer	28 degrees	47 minutes
Uranus in Capricorn	3 degrees	39 minutes
FIXED		
Mars in Aquarius	20 degrees	0 minutes
Node in Aquarius	24 degrees	03 minutes
Saturn in Aquarius	27 degrees	50 minutes
MUTABLE		
Venus in Sagittarius	7 degrees	02 minutes
Sun in Sagittarius	21 degrees	51 minutes
Mercury in Sagittarius	25 degrees	16 minutes
Pluto in Gemini	21 degrees	44 minutes

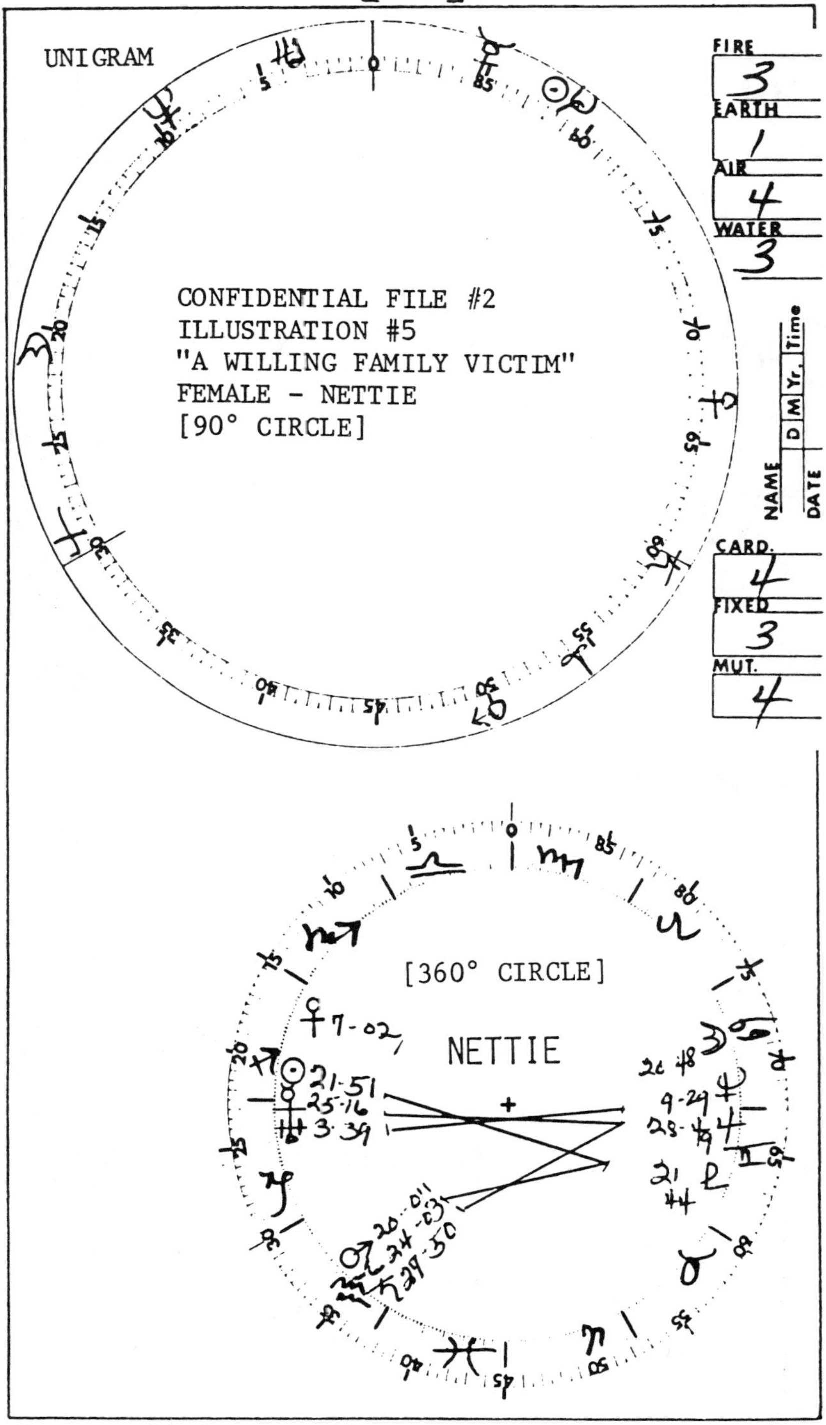
UNIGRAM
CONFIDENTIAL FILE #2
ILLUSTRATION #5
"A WILLING FAMILY VICTIM"
FEMALE - NETTIE
[90° CIRCLE]
FIRE 3
EARTH 1
AIR 4
WATER 3
NAME
DATE
D M Yr. Time
CARD. 4
FIXED 3
MUT. 4
[360° CIRCLE]
NETTIE

CONFIDENTIAL FILE #2
ILLUSTRATION #4 and #5
"A WILLING FAMILY VICTIM"
FEMALE - NETTIE

In the last year the old furnace has gone out and Nettie now spends a good deal of the day in bed under an electric blanket. There is no money to fix the furnace.

Nettie has found herself reading a lot of love pulps; she has over 300 romance paperbacks on the floor of her bedroom closet. Nettie loves a happy ending, something she cannot establish in life. [Sun = Venus/Neptune - Incurable Romantic]

Nettie is in her 70's. She lives on social security and a small savings left by her husband. All her life Nettie has done too much for the family without realizing it. She is just learning to place correct limits with her family.

Nettie's gentleness, sensitivity and family-oriented love is shown in the Moon/Jupiter/Neptune placements in CANCER! Neptune can idealize or waste the expansive Moon/Jupiter emotions.

MOON.............FEELINGS/EMOTIONS

JUPITER.........EXPANSION/HAPPINESS
NEPTUNE.........LIMITLESS

Sun/Pluto in Nettie's chart will always direct or dominate or be directed or dominated. Nettie's Sagittarian Sun with the weakening Venus/Neptune midpoint has always permitted herself to be dominated.

Sagittarius is mutable, easily pushed and the Venus/Neptune love midpoint is very idealistic. Venus contacts the family Moon by opposition. Thus an unrealistic love attitude in relation to the family was created.

SUN.........INDIVIDUAL SELF EXPRESSION
PLUTO.......DIRECT or DOMINATE
VENUS.......LOVE
NEPTUNE.....LIMITLESS/SENSITIVITY
MOON........FAMILY

Through the keywords you see easily the Moon/Venus (Family love) become idealized, then undermined through the contact to Neptune. It is quite understandable that Nettie developed an unrealistic concept of what family should do for each other.

Family members, when going through difficult times sought release from their problems by moving into Nettie's home. They came and went suddenly as is the nature of Uranus staying only until their problems were solved. During their stay they used both Nettie's meager funds plus her energies. The following natal structures show this sad condition.

SATURN (NATAL)

MOON.|...URANUS

KEYWORD INTERPRETATION

SATURN..........SEPARATION
MOON............FAMILY
URANUS..........SUDDEN

Sudden family separations!

MOON (NATAL)

MERCURY..|...SATURN/NODE

VENUS

KEYWORD INTERPRETATION

MOON......FAMILY
MERCURY...COMMUNICATION
SATURN....OPPRESSION/SEPARATION/
STABILIZATION
VENUS.....LOVE
NODE......CONTACT

Loving family (Moon-Venus) talk (Mercury) of possible stabilization or possible separation (Saturn). Saturn/Node can be oppressive contacts.

MOON (NATAL)

SUN/PLUTO. | .....MARS

KEYWORD INTERPRETATION

MOON.......FAMILY
SUN........MALE/INDIVIDUALITY
PLUTO......DIRECT OR DOMINATE
MARS.......MALE

Sun/Mars/Pluto would be an individual possessing intense energy. With the Moon (Family) contacting the Sun/Mars/Pluto you could say the individual would work intensely hard for the family.

Two years ago Nettie permitted her 40 year old daughter and son-in-law to move into her home until he found work; it was a disastrous mistake.

The money drain became impossible. Then Nettie learned she was to have surgery. At this point she confronted her son-in-law as to why in the many long months since he moved into her home had he not looked for work except twice.

He responded with crushing, filthy,

verbal abuse. Two days after the depreciating verbal attack Nettie took (50) tranquilizers. Her exhaustion from the anxiety over her family unhappiness, financial and health problems had been too much.

One obvious direction and several transits dramatically emphasize the Neptune confusion, emotional weakness, inability to draw lines and love disappointments that led to the suicide attempt.

DIRECTIONS

Directed Neptune to the natal Sun the year of the attempt shows weakened strength along with the possibility of dependent males being a cause of weakened strength.

This direction screamed for placing limits and added rest. With the extra family members in the home Nettie, instead of delegating, was working twice as hard. She did not have time to rest nor time to develop the Neptune creativity that was necessary to effectively handle this transit.

Age, economic condition or environment will not withhold manifestation when the planetary energies present themselves; there is always an outlet available at that time for effective use of those planetary energies.

Nettie, for instance, even in the 70 age bracket, could have satisfied this urgent Neptune creative development need simply by taking time to appreciate beauty, reading, listening to music or becoming more uniquely interested in her knitting, sewing, crocheting - or one of her hobbies.

Reading her love pulps during this period would have been better than over-taxing her strength doing jobs she failed to have the family do. If Nettie could not learn how to delegate and set limits, then rest must take presidence through this Neptune period.

With Neptune directions and transits the mind must be able to be clear, enthusiastic and buoyant in some effective way to handle the heightened sensitivity and offset the easily weakened bodily energies.

TRANSITS

Transits for the week and the day of the tragic suicide attempt set a special scene!

Transiting Uranus to natal Mars with

a natal Uranus/Neptune midpoint brought the following energies to the moment in time:

KEYWORDS

MARS........ENERGY/BRUTALITY/MALE
URANUS......SUDDEN/DEVELOPMENT
NEPTUNE.....WEAKNESS/CONFUSION/CREATIVITY

INTERPRETATION:

Mars/Uranus/Neptune brought several energies from a male [Mars] to Nettie. They were: sudden energy, aggressive, brutal energy and weak and confused energy. Mars/Uranus tried to be the sudden drawing of lines. Nettie confronted her son-in-law suddenly, rather aggressively as to why he was not looking daily for work.

Unfortunately, Neptune destroyed the effective Mars/Uranus confrontation. Neptune brought weakness and confusion causing a sudden upset and a brutal attack. [Mars/Uranus]

A daily calm reminder of the need for more financial support made when both the daughter and the son-in-law were together would have been more appropriate with these energies. This plan of consistent routine and method would more effectively pave the way for Neptune co-operation with aggressive Mars/

Uranus energy.

Transiting Neptune midpointing Venus/ Uranus reveals the sudden disappointment in love. Loving Venus contacting the family Moon in the natal chart signified family love. This loving Moon/Venus must have been devastated by the sudden crushing Uranus/Neptune verbal abuse.

Transiting Neptune contacting natal Moon/Mars again weakened and confused the emotions and energy causing an untimely confrontation. The Moon/Neptune emotions must surely have excited and upset the Mars energy igniting the suicide attempt.

Transiting Mars midpointing Mars/ Saturn indicated possible male cruelty as well as extremely frustrated energy.

Transiting Mars to Neptune was a major transit of disappointment, confusion, misguided energy and even possible cunning and enmity or hatred. The son-in-law would never have dared to speak in such a manner to Nettie had her daughter been present!

Transiting Mars had recently midpointed sudden Uranus and undermining Neptune several days before the attempt accentuating heightened sensitivity, upsets and weakened strength.

Dour Saturn midpointed Mercury/Venus bringing heavy thoughts in regard to love denial. Nettie must have felt tremendously rejected!

Oppressive Saturn also midpointed Mars/Uranus bringing its share of difficult psychological tension to overcome.

And lastly on the day of the attempt, transiting Sun midpointed Moon/Neptune filling Nettie to overflowing with the cruel exploitation by her loved ones along with great sensitive moodiness.

It is not difficult to understand Nettie's frenzied moment as she devoured 50 tranquilizers.

IMPORTANT NOTE:
Nettie recovered. Out of her torment came a new Nettie. Recall her natal Sun/Pluto telling us Nettie will experience many transformations regarding her individuality!

Saturn represents conscience and limitation as well as the 'stabilization/separation' emphasis we have been speaking of.

Had Nettie not imposed so much limitation on herself through an unworthy, duty-bound conscience she would have had more strength in which to cope with the Directed Neptune to the natal Sun.

It is vital to become aware that Saturn 'conscience' and Saturn 'family' need just as strong limits placed as you would place with Neptune creativity and Neptune compassion.

The Saturn 'martyr' is as ineffective behavior-wise as the Neptune 'escapist'. In both cases there is great victimizing!

KATHY

AN ATTEMPTER!

LOVE VICTIMIZATION!

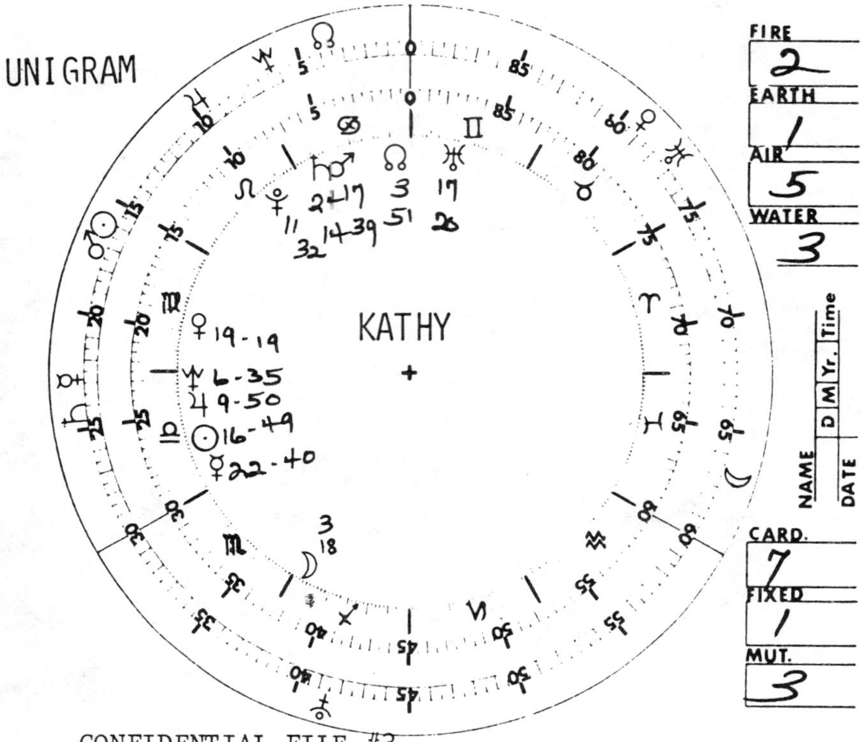

CONFIDENTIAL FILE #3
ILLUSTRATION # 6
"AN ATTEMPTER"
FEMALE - KATHY

CARDINAL		
Node in Cancer	3 degrees	51 minutes
Mars in Cancer	17 degrees	39 minutes
Saturn in Cancer	24 degrees	14 minutes
Neptune in Libra	6 degrees	35 minutes
Jupiter in Libra	9 degrees	50 minutes
Sun in Libra	16 degrees	49 minutes
Mercury in Libra	22 degrees	40 minutes
FIXED		
Pluto in Leo	11 degrees	32 minutes
MUTABLE		
Uranus in Gemini	17 degrees	20 minutes
Venus in Virgo	19 degrees	19 minutes
Moon in Sagittarius	3 degrees	18 minutes

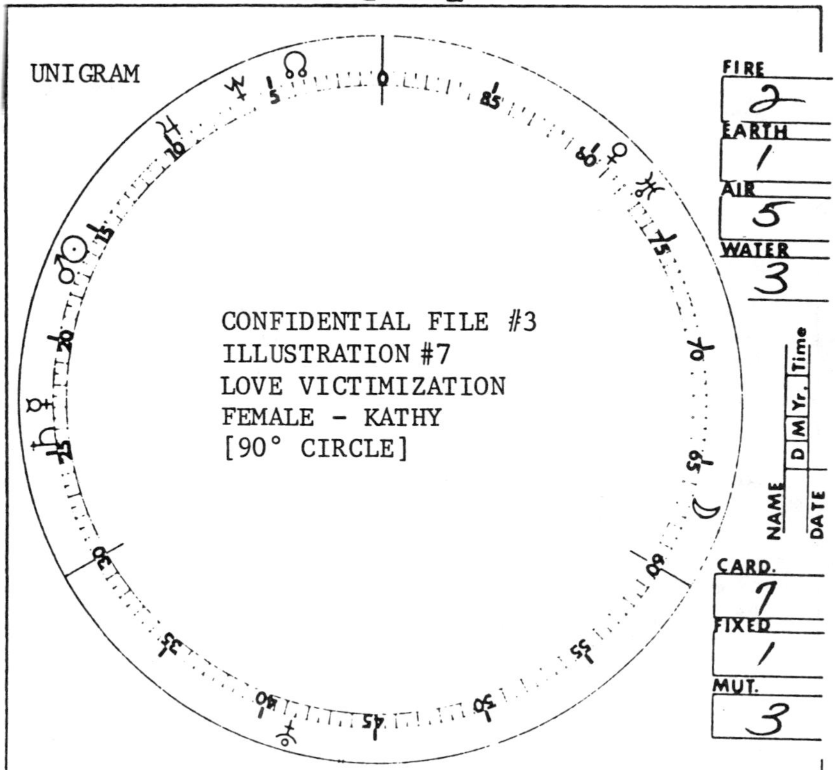
UNIGRAM
CONFIDENTIAL FILE #3
ILLUSTRATION #7
LOVE VICTIMIZATION
FEMALE - KATHY
[90° CIRCLE]
FIRE
2
EARTH
1
AIR
5
WATER
3
NAME
D
M
Yr.
Time
DATE
CARD.
7
FIXED
1
MUT.
3

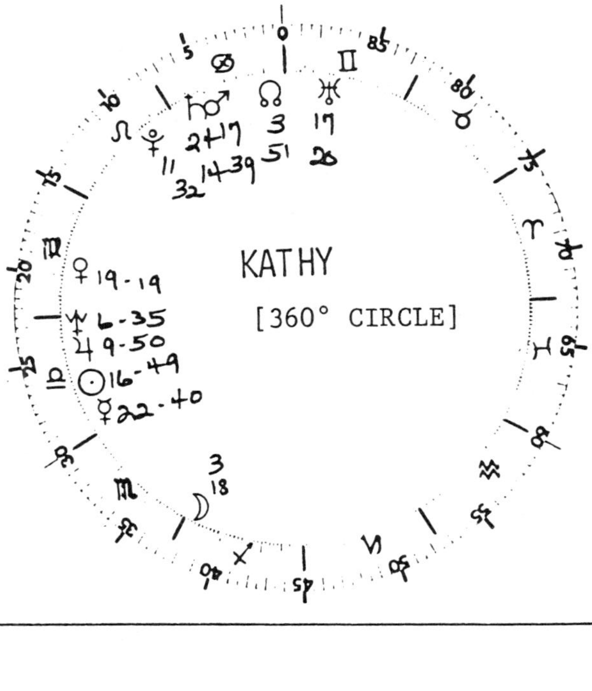
KATHY
[360° CIRCLE]
19-19
6-35
9-50
16-49
22-40

CONFIDENTIAL FILE #3
ILLUSTRATION #6 and #7
"AN ATTEMPTER"
FEMALE - KATHY

Three years ago Kathy was rushed to emergency. She was violent and had to be restrained. They pumped her stomach and the volunteer talked with her for 2½ hours.

She was very cold and her teeth chattered when she finally gave her consent to the Doctor to be admitted to the psychiatric ward for counseling. It was Kathy's 2nd suicide attempt in the last month.

Two years before the suicide attempt Kathy met a fantastically exciting man. The romantic directions that brought this man so suddenly into her life were Directed Uranus to natal Sun/Mars (Male) and Directed Venus (Love) to natal Moon (Feelings). There was an irresistible quality about him that fascinated her.

He was everything she had ever wanted in a man. As Kathy stated, 'he made her feel like a woman' which was a nebulous statement made by thousands of women long before Kathy's time.

She was saying in essence, "My intensely romantic natal Venus-Uranus has found through its idealistic Moon/Neptune midpoint love perfection!

The only catch was that her ideal lovemate had quite a few other women and he did not keep this secret from her; in fact, he reminded her quite often of her competition. (Sun/Mars/Moon configuration can indicate emotional cruelty from a male).

KEYWORDS:

SUN..........MALE
MARS.........ENERGY/AGGRESSION/MALE
MOON.........EMOTIONS

Kathy felt he would change in his feeling if they could only live together for awhile. So she went against her very structured emotions (Moon/Jupiter/Saturn) and strong principles (Moon/Mars) and left home. (Moon/Mars is also a very passionate, impetuous woman.

Kathy forced her lover's hand and moved into his apartment. He told her from the start he did not want this type of relationship with her.

But Kathy was so intensely in love with him that she convinced herself she would change him. (Pluto = Venus/Node indicated a very intense love contact or a fateful love contact.

KEYWORDS:

PLUTO.........INTENSITY/FATE
VENUS.........LOVE/ART
CONTACT.......FRIENDS/ACQUAINTANCES/LOVERS

Kathy became pregnant and had her lover's baby. When he menaced her by consistently telling her he was going to leave her she reacted with suicide threats. (Venus/Pluto can be fanatic and manipulative in love.)

Another year went by. Kathy had been a good nurse and she wanted to return to work but she could not even handle part-time shifts consistently; she was always anxious and exhausted from the emotional turmoil she was constantly under.

Because she could not draw lines or make a decision to leave her parasitic lover, Kathy's Directed Moon contacting her natal Neptune became confused, disorderly, chaotic domestic life.

Transiting Uranus brought the condition to a head when the 'sudden development' planet contacted Jupiter/Neptune and Venus/Uranus midpoints and started a series of sudden, devastating, love disappointments!

Her lover became more open with his

love affairs. He kept Kathy informed about his 'exciting other women'. He wanted out of the relationship with her. In regard to the baby he expressed his feelings in one sentence, "Do what you want with the baby; I could care less."

Transiting Neptune to her natal Sun/Mars and Sun/Pluto midpoints had done a good job undermining her energy through her male lover.

KEYWORDS:
SUN........MALE
MARS...... MALE
PLUTO/NEPTUNE....INTENSE UNDERMINING

She could not bear the thought of life without him. Nor could she envision returning home to her domineering (Moon/Mars) deeply-religious (Moon/Jupiter/Saturn) mother; so, she did the only thing she felt was left for her to do.

She ingested 37 tranquilizers; each tablet containing a fine, light, yellow, practically odorless powder indicated by the prescription to be symtomatic of relief of anxiety. By taking 37 tablets Kathy hoped for complete relief of all anxiety - death!

On that day of confusion and dire

unhappiness Kathy had the following transits aggravating the Neptune directions already discussed:

TRANSITING URANUS to VENUS/NEPTUNE
<u>KEYWORDS:</u>
URANUS................SUDDEN
VENUS/NEPTUNE........LOVE DISAPPOINTMENT

TRANSITING SATURN to MOON/MARS/SUN
<u>KEYWORDS:</u>
MARS/SATURN..........CRUELTY FROM MARS MALE
MOON/MARS/SATURN.... EMOTIONAL CRUELTY

TRANSITING MARS to SUN/MARS
<u>KEYWORDS:</u>
SUN..........MALE
MARS.........MALE
SUN/MARS.....ATTACK

TRANSITING SUN to SATURN
<u>KEYWORDS:</u>
SUN..........MALE
SATURN.......DESPAIR/DEPRESSION/CRUELTY

TRANSITING MERCURY to NEPTUNE
<u>KEYWORDS:</u>
MERCURY..........COMMUNICATION
NEPTUNE..........DISAPPOINTMENT

Her lover found her, rushed her to the

hospital emergency and left her.

One month later she was back again in that same emergency room after taking 98 tablets of a more potent tranquilizer. This time she accepted the hospital's psychiatric help after her stolmach was pumped.

She went from the hospital rehabilitation, with her baby, back home to her Mother. It was three years before she adjusted and stopped having Neptune 'panic' attacks. (Transiting Neptune = Venus/Uranus and Transiting Saturn = Venus/Uranus were responsible for the attacks.

KEYWORDS:

VENUS/URANUS/NEPTUNE .....Sudden/Love/Disappointment
SATURN/VENUS/URANUS......Sudden/Love/Separation or Sudden/Love/Despair

Once her attack was so bad she had to leave a restaurant so she wouldn't start screaming. At the end of the three years the adjustment had been made. It was in December that her mother proudly told a neighbor that Kathy had gotten part-time work at a nursing home and Kathy's X-mas preparation had already been completed in early November.

Kathy had made it. The next time she left home she would do it, hopefully, under more stable planetary aspects. Unreliable, romantic Uranus would not so easily draw Kathy into a sudden love affair again!

JOAN AND SAMARIAN

TRAGEDY!

ENVIRONMENTAL VICTIMIZATION!

UNIGRAM

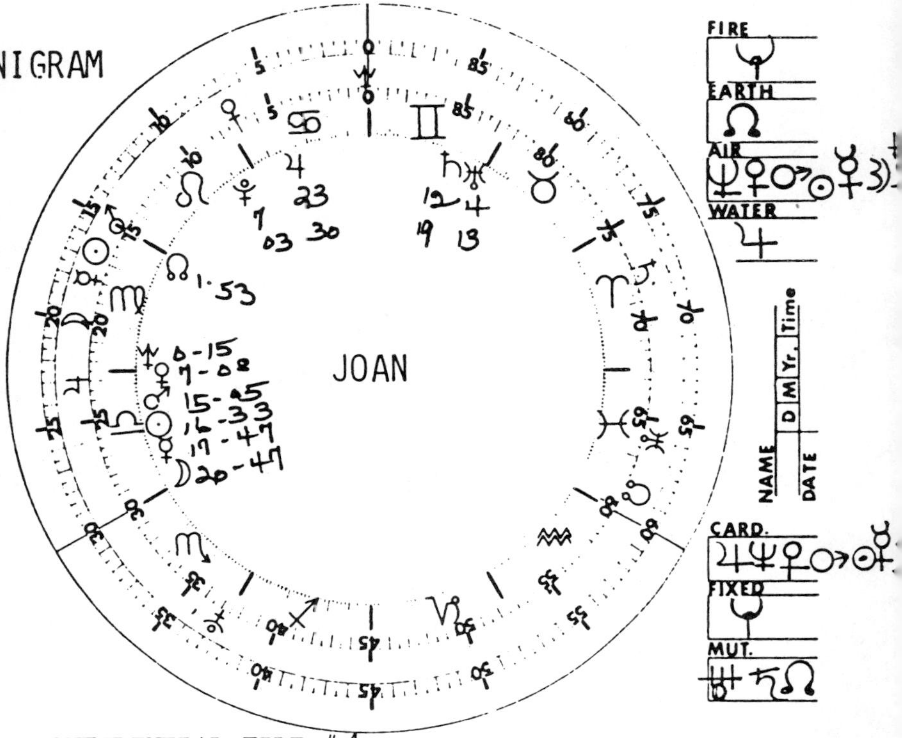

CONFIDENTIAL FILE # 4
ILLUSTRATION # 8
LOVE DESTINY FULFILLED!
FEMALE - JOAN

<u>CARDINAL</u>		
Jupiter in Cancer	23 degrees	30 minutes
Neptune in Libra	0 degrees	15 minutes
Venus in Libra	7 degrees	8 minutes
Mars in Libra	15 degrees	5 minutes
Sun in Libra	16 degrees	33 minutes
Mercury in Libra	17 degrees	47 minutes
Moon in Libra	20 degrees	47 minutes
<u>FIXED</u>		
Pluto in Leo	7 degrees	03 minutes
<u>MUTABLE</u>		
Uranus in Gemini	4 degrees	13 minutes
Saturn in Gemini	12 degrees	19 minutes
Node in Virgo	1 degree	53 minutes

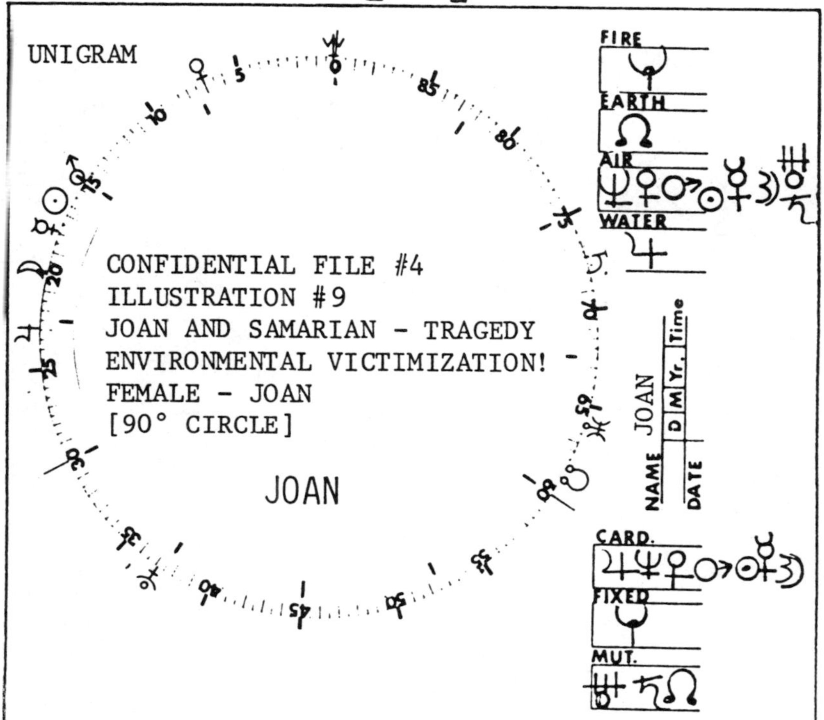
UNIGRAM
CONFIDENTIAL FILE #4
ILLUSTRATION #9
JOAN AND SAMARIAN - TRAGEDY
ENVIRONMENTAL VICTIMIZATION!
FEMALE - JOAN
[90° CIRCLE]
JOAN
FIRE
EARTH
AIR
WATER
NAME
JOAN
DATE
D
M
Yr.
Time
CARD.
FIXED
MUT.

JOAN

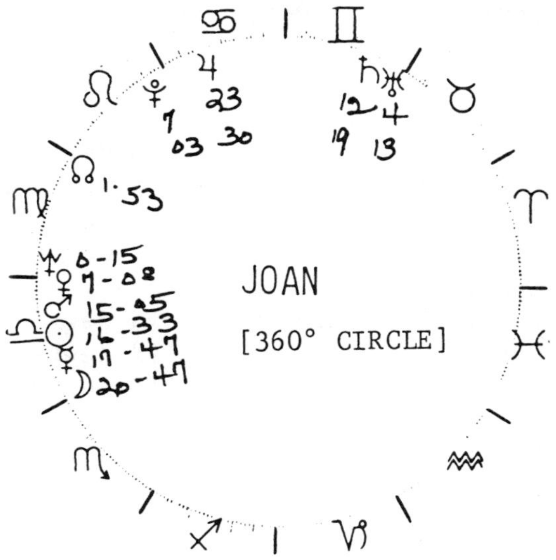
JOAN
[360° CIRCLE]
1.53
0-15
7-08
15-25
16-33
17-47
20-47

UNIGRAM

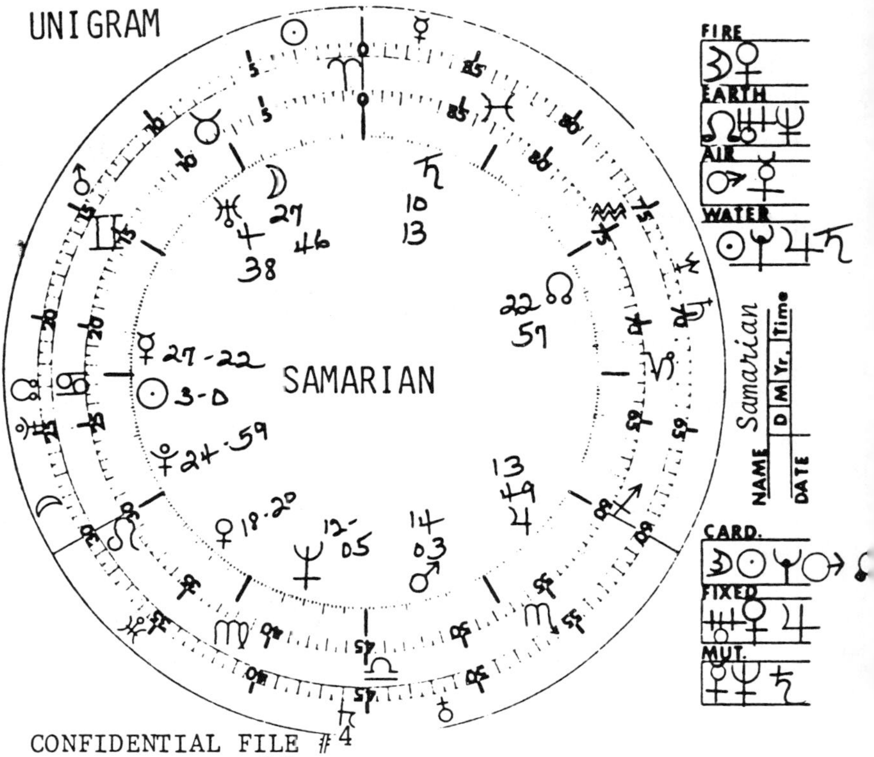

CONFIDENTIAL FILE #4
ILLUSTRATION #10
LOVE DESTINY FULFILLED!
MALE - SAMARIAN

CARDINAL

Moon in Aries	27 degrees	46 minutes
Sun in Cancer	3 degrees	0 minutes
Pluto in Cancer	24 degrees	59 minutes
Mars in Libra	14 degrees	03 minutes
Node in Capricorn	22 degrees	57 minutes

FIXED

Uranus in Taurus	4 degrees	38 minutes
Venus in Leo	18 degrees	20 minutes
Jupiter in Scorpio	13 degrees	49 minutes

MUTABLE

Mercury in Gemini	27 degrees	22 minutes
Neptune in Virgo	12 degrees	05 minutes
Saturn in Pisces	10 degrees	13 minutes

UNIGRAM

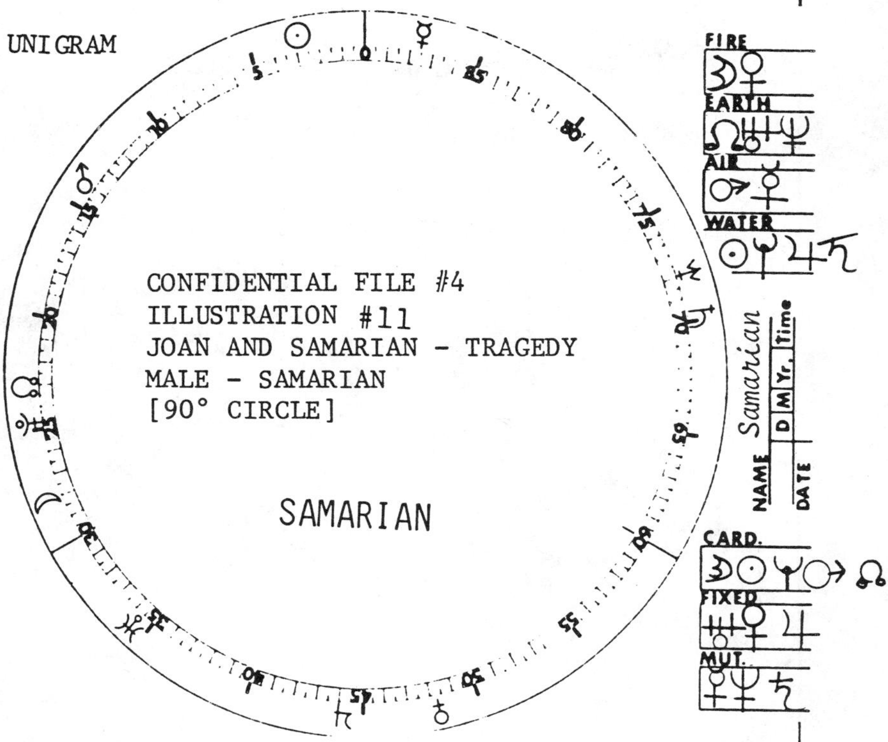

SAMARIAN

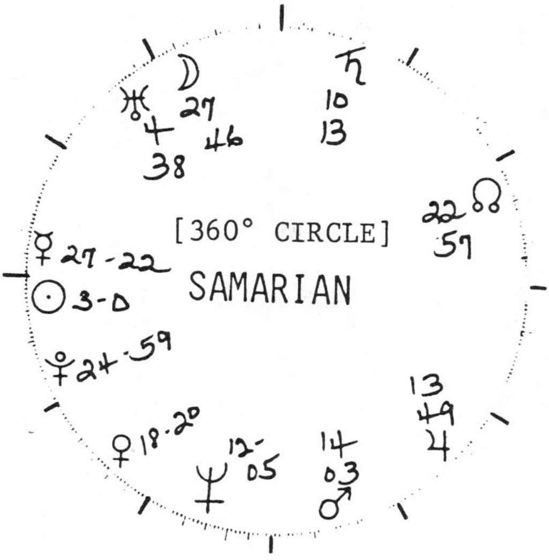

SYNASTRY - CHART COMPARISON
JOAN AND SAMARIAN

UNIGRAM

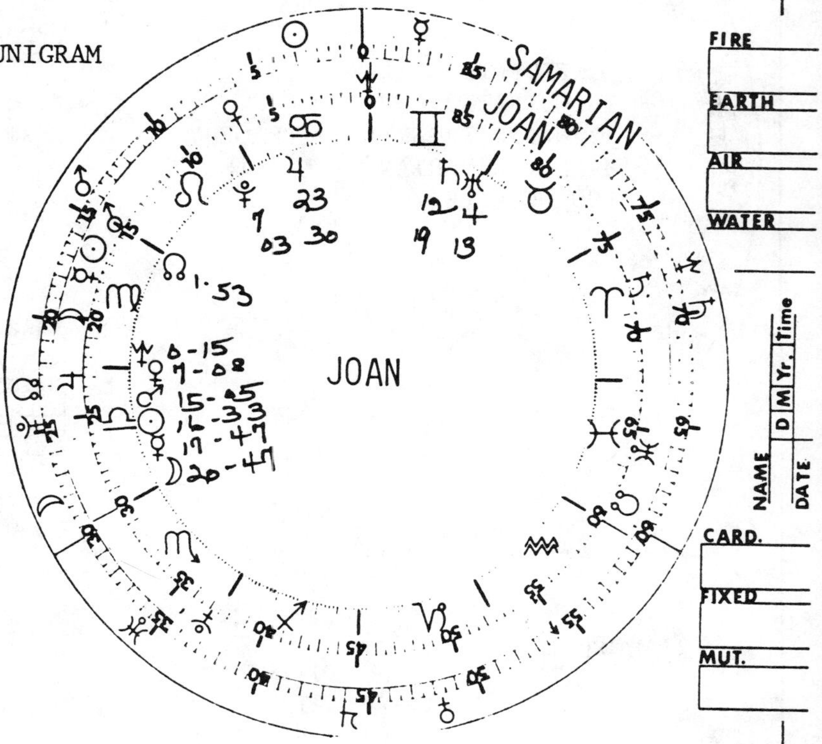

CONFIDENTIAL FILE #4
ILLUSTRATION #12
SYNASTRY - CHART COMPARISON
JOAN AND SAMARIAN

CONFIDENTIAL FILE # 4
ILLUSTRATION #8-9-10-11-12
LOVE DESTINY FULFILLED!
JOAN - FEMALE
SAMARIAN - MALE

There are many circumstances and conditions that shape the love destiny of an individual. You must deal with heredity, economic conditions, environment and lastly free will.

The following confidential file - the love stoy of Joan and Samarian emphasizes the essential early environmental dynamics or underlying forces that played such a vital part in the creation of their concept of love.

This confidential file dramatically points up the fact that an astrological interpretation is worth more intrinsic value with a complete and thorough understanding of the early environment that shaped each partner under analysis.

The following two birthdays are of a female in love and a male in love, Joan and Samarian.

These two vital human beings met, fell suddenly in love, married quickly after meeting, lived a violently tormented life together; then both died just as violently and tragically together.

The broad spectrum of frustrated planetary energies ignited through the coming together of this love relationship forced these two people to grow together again an impossible 'separateness'. This 'separateness' occurred as a result of environmental (Ascendant) rearing differences.

Sorrow at the inquest of Joan and Samarian was undeniably ignorance; their destinies had been beautifully fulfilled when viewed from their miraculous accomplishment resulting from their planetary struggles.

Our story begins when Transiting Jupiter contacted Samrian's natal Uranus and he is suddenly released from his native Turkey and sent with his brothers to the United States to begin their psychiatric practice.

The trip to the United States was Samarian's first time away from home. Up until that time he had lived his entire life with his hard-working Armenian family in a very modest home.

On the wall in the kitchen of that home was a poem that quietly substantiated the omnipotence of the male. The poem read as follows:

Shifting The Sun
By Diana Der Hovanessian

When your father dies, say the Irish
You lose your umbrella against bad weather
May his sun be your light, say the Armenians

When your father dies, say the Welsh
You sink a foot deeper into the earth
May you inherit his light, say the Armenians

When your father dies, say the Canadians
You run out of excuses
May you inherit his sun, say the Armenians

When you father dies, say the French
You become your own father
May you stand up in his light say the
Armenians

When your father dies, say the Indians
He comes back as the thunder
May you inherit his light, say the Armenians

When your father dies, say the Russians
He takes your childhood with him
May you inherit his light, say the Armenians

When your father dies, say the English
You join his club you vowed you wouldn't
May you inherit his sun say the Armenians

When your father dies, say the Armenians
Your sun shifts forever
And you walk in his light.

In Samarian's home the females were much loved and protected by the male members; their role was clearly defined as submissive, non-intellectual and non-worldly. The life of the female was the 'family' and the 'home'. Even in this, her area of life, the male had the final decision. Only recently had her culture permitted her to go without a veil.

Under Transiting Jupiter to his natal Uranus, Samiarian was not only released to a wonderful, prosperous new country but the Jupiter/Uranus contact also brought an exciting new romance into his life!

At a peaceful, happy Jupiter/Uranus church buffet in his new country, Samarian met Joan and later married her. Much later, under violently tragic aspects, a bizarre courtroom scene separated them forever!

The birth chart of both Joan and Samarian reveal two very uniquely individualistic people.

Joan was a determined, independent strong-willed individual [Sun/Mars/Mercury combination]. She worked hard at her marriage. She tried to be a perfect wife for Samarian. She loved her children. Her loyalities to her family were deeply felt [Jupiter in Cancer].

Despite the great effort put toward complete domesticity Joan's drive, her dedication, ambition and talent would not let her be held captive by the home. Her strong German rearing had encouraged not only family loyalty but individualistic career accomplishment. Her brother was a doctor, her sister was studying to be a nurse and Joan was reared to find her 'uniqueness' also. Her three strong planets in Libra needed many companions in the outside world to recognize and benefit from her intellectual abilities.

Eventually Joan had to face the fact that her home and family could not ever be the beginning and end of her existence. She needed to create a family of man. [Jupiter in Cancer with the intellectual Libra emphasis - Mars/Mercury/Sun in Libra] Joan had to return to school for her masters.

This serious decision was the beginning of a Pluto transformation. Joan would one day be appointed Co-ordinator and Nutritionist of a Senior Citizens program where she would at last begin to realize her ambitions - if only for but a sweet moment in time!

Samarian, Joan's husband, also had a very strong intellectual bent; possessing the same Sun/Mercury/Mars combination as his wife. The difference being the sign location; Samarian's Sun was in domestic, home oriented Cancer, Mercury in high-strung Gemini, and Mars in intellectual Libra.

Along with this dynamic emotional-intellectual energy Samarian possessed enormous discipline, tenacity and endurance. His basic make-up was cold and unfeeling.

Samarian held a fanatic adherence to his religous principles; they were his life. All his strength and fanaticism can be read through his Sun/Saturn/Pluto combination. The basic individual [Sun] was intensely [Pluto] disciplined [Saturn]. Strangely enough Joan also had this same combination in her Saturn = Sun/Pluto midpoint which told something of her husband's [Sun] discipline as well as her own character.

Environment had reared Samarian to view himself successful as a man - only if he completely controlled his wife and children. Samarian's relious outlook would be Joan's greatest obstacle to her career.

Joan had to succeed in a career by working against a religious bias that would see her husband as a failure if she became independent outside of the home. Nothing could change this environmental religious intensity that flowed with a great intensity through Samarian's veins [So = Sa/Pl].

Samarian made Joan pay for everything that involved the building of her career. She had to pay him mileage for the use of his car when she went back to school for her masters degree. Then he insisted she pay for the babysitter for the children out of her own funds.

Along with this chronic frustration he inflicted location moves upon her. Everytime she developed close friends or advanced in her development outside of the home he insisted they move. Many of these moves were to the outskirts of town; rural areas. She was always left without a car; completely isolated.

This is so easily understood as you see Samarian's natal Saturn suffocatingly oppress Joan's natal Jupiter expansion. Effectively Samarian's Saturn could have stabilized and made profitable Joan's Jupiter career but this was not the story.

Samarian's behavior only acted as a catalyst for her ever-growing drive.

Directed Pluto was responsible for her vigorous career effort as it contacted her natal Mars energy, her Sun individuality, her Mercury mind, her Moon emotions and Jupiter, her planet of opportunities. This Direction occurred in the nine years that followed their marriage.

As Joan became more totally emotionally independent she could see her way clear to making a very important decision; divorce. [Directed Saturn was contacting her natal Sun (husband) and her Mercury (mind).]

Joan filed for divorce. Samarian was awarded custody of the children; the 12 year old chose to live Samarian and both parents felt the children should be together. The court had proclaimed both people fit parents.

The filing of the divorce and the two-year period in which it became final showed obviously in Samarian's chart: Directed Moon [wife/emotions] contacted Saturn [separation] and Neptune [dissolution and confusion]. This was a configuration of great, mental-emotional suffering for Samarian.

Two other major directions were in evidence during this same divorce period. Directed Neptune, followed closely by Directed Saturn, (See Saturn-Neptune conjunction in 90° circle) contacted the Node giving Samarian a great sense of lonliness and isolation.

Directed Neptune and Saturn contacting Pluto brought a note of rebelliousness, violence and confusion to the termination of the relationship.

At the end of this two-year period of very heavy undermining, ruthless directions as described above Samarian again came to the courthouse for the final custody hearing. He was leaving town and there was a question as to whether he could take the children with him.

Samarian now beheld himself with a Pluto tenseness and Neptune confusion in regard to the eyes of his culture. Should he lose custody of his children he would have lost not only his wife but his entire family. This was the loss of complete control of his family. He would no longer be a man. He would be nothing at all!

Neptune made him feel that his woman [Joan] sitting across from him in the courtroom was trying to take away his heritage .... his manhood. He was right in his decision about what to do. It was the only thing he could do. [Joan] was responsible for his depreciation as a man.

Joan had no idea of the Neptune twisted mental condition of Samarian as she faced him in the courtroom waiting for the decision on the custody of the children.

For some time Samarian was strangely silent and then in one horrifying explosion of violence brought about by this incredible build up of cultural frustration he lunged forward and grossly attacked [Joan] in the presence of all in the crowded courtroom.

With sudden Pluto animal strength in his hands and arms he buried a knife to the hilt of its six inch blade into her chest, her neck, her head, her arms and her hands.

The utterly senseless act committed in ferocious bizarre rage was done.

It took [Joan] 30 minutes to die. She died slowly and with excruciating pain; even in the process of her death he controlled and frustrated her. His planets contacting hers did not permit her an easy death.

Samarian appeared lifeless and disorganized [Neptune] from the utterly senseless act. There was no longer panic in his make-up. The irrational, barbaric urge that had seized him had taken its victim. He was at last free of ever losing complete control of his wife and children.

Samarian was led out of the courtroom and taken to a cell to live the rest of his life with the Pluto violence of his insane act.

Two days later Samarian hanged himself in his cell. Two days following the hanging he was cremated and laid to rest next to the cremated remains of his life partner.

LAURA

AN ATTEMPTER!

RELIGIOUS CONCEPT VICTIMIZATION!

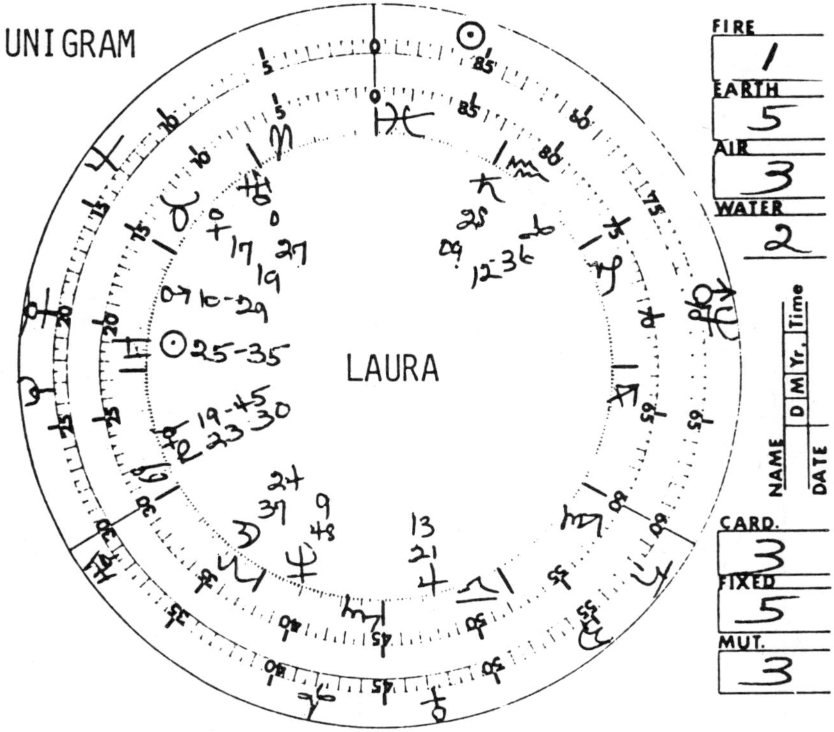

CONFIDENTIAL FILE #5
ILLUSTRATION #13
"AN ATTEMPTER"
FEMALE - LAURA

CARDINAL		
Mercury in Cancer	19 degrees	45 minutes
Pluto in Cancer	23 degrees	30 minutes
Jupiter in Libra	13 degrees	21 minutes
FIXED		
Uranus in Taurus	1 degree	27 minutes
Venus in Taurus	17 degrees	19 minutes
Moon in Leo	24 degrees	37 minutes
Node in Aquarius	12 degrees	36 minutes
Saturn in Aquarius	28 degrees	07 minutes
MUTABLE		
Mars in Gemini	10 degrees	29 minutes
Sun in Gemini	25 degrees	35 minutes
Neptune in Virgo	9 degrees	48 minutes

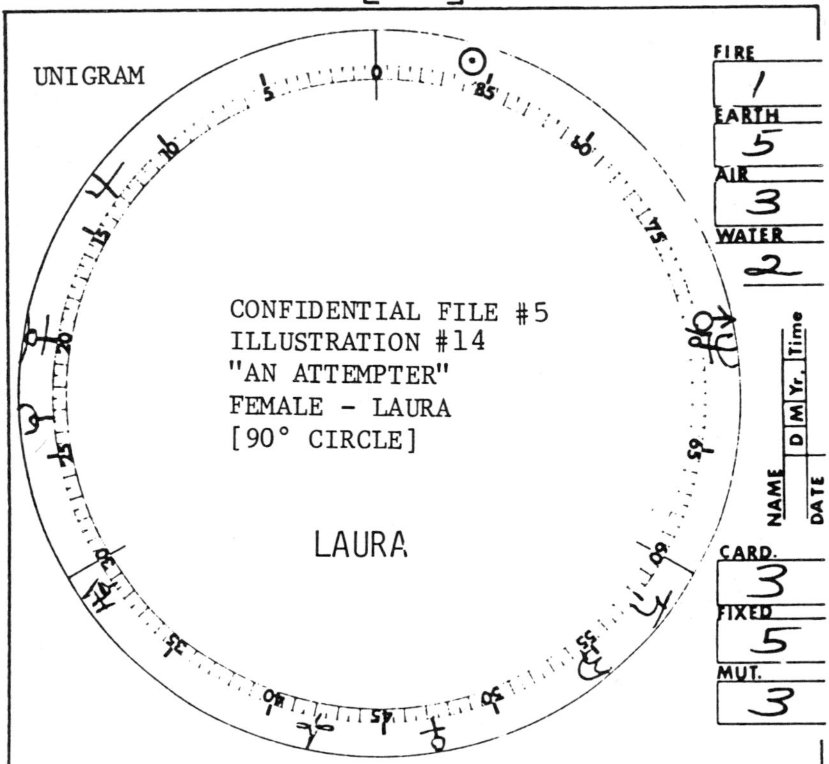
UNIGRAM
CONFIDENTIAL FILE #5
ILLUSTRATION #14
"AN ATTEMPTER"
FEMALE - LAURA
[90° CIRCLE]
LAURA
FIRE
1
EARTH
5
AIR
3
WATER
2
NAME
DATE
D M Yr. Time
CARD.
3
FIXED
5
MUT.
3

LAURA

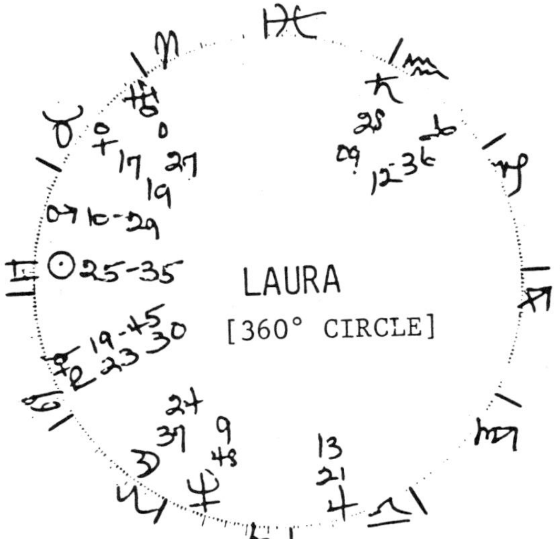
LAURA
[360° CIRCLE]

CONFIDENTIAL FILE #5
ILLUSTRATION #13 & #14
"THAT FRIDAY NIGHT!"
FEMALE - LAURA

Twenty-five years of marriage with its love and sacrifice had been a joy for Laura. [Mocn/Jupiter/Saturn].

KEYWORDS: [LAURA'S NATAL CHART]

MOON/SATURN.........FAMILY/SACRIFICE
JUPITER.............JOY/HAPPINESS

Laura had always been possessive in caring for her husband Jack. [Possessive Venus in Taurus and domineering Moon in Leo]. She always had to keep after Jack to see the dentist, go with him for a new suit, find his missing gloves in the winter; he was worse than either of the children.

LAURA'S
SUN[NATAL MIDPOINTS]

MARS-NEPTUNE..|....JUPITER

KEYWORD INTERPRETATION:

MARS..............MALE
NEPTUNE...........DEPENDENT
JUPITER...........HAPPINESS
INTERPRETATION: HAPPINESS THROUGH DEPENDENT HUSBAND!

NATAL SUN
REPRESENTS HUSBAND
IN LAURA'S CHART

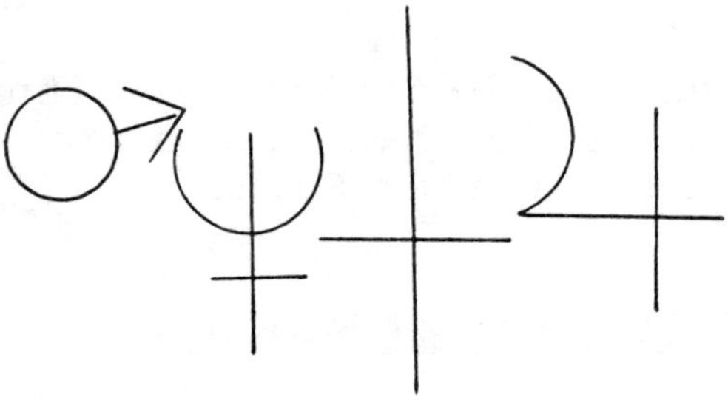

INTERPRETATION: HAPPINESS [JUPITER] THROUGH DEPENDANT [MARS/NEPTUNE] HUSBAND -

CONFIDENTIAL FILE #5 - LAURA
<u>RELIGIOUS CONCEPT VICTIMIZATION</u>

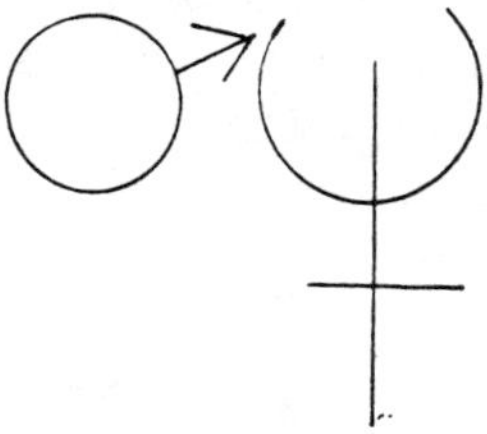

NATAL MARS
REPRESENTS
HUSBAND IN
LAURA'S CHART

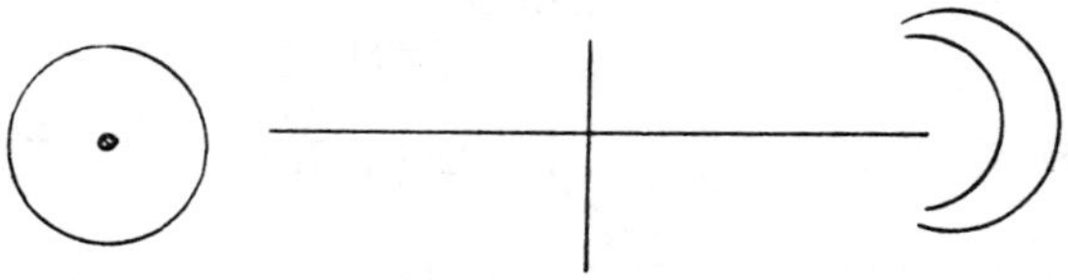

MARS/NEPTUNE......DEPENDENT
SUN...............MALE
MOON..............EMOTIONS

INTERPRETATION: EMOTIONALLY DEPENDENT HUSBAND OR EMOTIONALLY DEPENDENT ON HUSBAND

In one area of his life though Jack was not a little boy; he was a hard-working, duty-bound provider. This you see through the Sun = Saturn/Pluto midpoint, an intense (Pluto) disciplined (Saturn) male (Sun).

Laura always remembered that dedicated part of Jack's make-up. Her Mercury/Pluto mind was never quite free of analyzing the emotional trauma of that tragic Friday night!

<u>KEYWORDS: [LAURA'S NATAL MIDPOINT]</u>

MERCURY...THE MIND/THINKING/COMMUNICATION
PLUTO.....ANALYSIS/INTENSITY

INTERPRETATION: MERCURY/PLUTO MIND COULD NOT THROW OFF OR FREE ITSELF OF THE PAST!

She was so unprepared for the discovery Directed Uranus to Sun/Jupiter brought. [Sun/Jupiter represented the happy husband and Uranus represented the sudden change.]

It was snowing lightly that night of the discovery. They dropped Carrie and Jim home as was their usual Frinight custom. The show had been fair but somewhere between the show and the sandwiches at the restaurant the strangeness started to set in.

Jack was unusually quiet and Laura's thoughts amazingly forced her to tie this quiet in with the very beginning of that strange pattern of quiet spells that began several years ago - the spring their friend Jim had been hospitalized and his wife Carrie had been so overwrought.

That was the year Laura pushed Jack, along with her, to be a helpmate for Carrie through this difficult period. Jack took Carrie to the hospital, to the store, to the dentist with the kids etc. After all Laura had known Carrie since high school for some 29 years. Wasn't that what good friends were for?

<u>KEYWORD SHOCK!</u>

DIRECTIONS FOR LAURA THE YEAR SHE AND JACK HELPED CARRIE! [LAURA'S NATAL]

DIRECTED NEPTUNE TO NATAL MERCURY
NEPTUNE...........DECEPTION
MERCURY...........COMMUNICATION

DIRECTED JUPITER TO NATAL MOON
JUPITER..........HAPPINESS
MOON.............FEMALE

DIRECTED VENUS/NODE
MIDPOINT TO THE NATAL SUN
VENUS/NODE............LOVE CONTACT
SUN...................MALE/HUSBAND IN LAURA'S CHART

INTERPRETATION: [KEYWORD SHOCK!]

Neptune/Mercury told of the untruthful or deception communication. Laura's philosophic Jupiter had truly tried to help the Moon - female friend. But most astounding was the Venus/Node midpoint to the Sun interpretation. That midpoint occurred the year that the quiet spells between Laura and Jack began. Laura's Sun husband had pulled away from her that year so obviously Laura was not the Venus/Node midpoint love contact. Someone else was! Neptune had clouded the Mercury thinking and Laura did not recognize the deception at the time.

Laura was meant to discover the secret under Uranus/Sun/Jupiter that Friday night. The garage doors closed behind them. They got out in silence and the sound of the key in the door was the next grating noise in Laura's intense thinking.

He closed the backdoor behind them. "What's wrongJack? What is it?" She knew he wanted her to ask.

It was a scene more melodramatic than the movie they'd just seen, but Laura didn't feel like an actress. Her ears suddenly ached and she felt nauseous as Transiting Saturn brought a clear picture of her marriage lovelife to her through its contact to her natal Venus.

"There's something I have to tell you." His face was gray-white and his eyes were frightened. Laura saw weakness instead of the little-boy quality she had always loved.

"What is it Jack?" Silence again and then he destroyed her 25 year myth of happily married love with his answer.

"Carrie and I are in love. We've decided we want to get married as soon as possible. Carrie is going to tell Jim tonight."

Saturn reality had pointed up the love affair during Jack's frequent absences in the last five years; the pattern she had perpetuated to help her dear friend through a trying time in life.

Transiting Uranus to Laura's natal Pluto suddenly freed her of male deception through a transformation.

TRANSITING URANUS TO ....

PLUTO [NATAL]

JUPITER..|.....URANUS
MOON....|.....SUN

MARS/NEPTUNE

KEYWORDS:

JUPITER/URANUS..........RELEASE
MOON/SUN................MALE/FEMALE
MARS/NEPTUNE............MALE DECEPTION
PLUTO...................TRANSFORMATION

Had Laura's Directed Jupiter to her Moon/Saturn expanded her duty-bound responsibiliities to such a point where she actually pushed Jack into another woman's life?

Laura had never turned to anything but her religion (Mars/Neptune religious emotionalism) but now this event suddenly brought an aching lonliness that required erasing. She acquired a new habit to do this erasing - alcohol (Again Mars/Neptune in the negative).

KEYWORDS:

MOON/JUPITER/SATURN.....STRONG RELIGIOUS PRINCIPLES
MARS/NEPTUNE............RELIGIOUS EMOTIONALISM VS ESCAPISM

The alcohol pushed Laura into 'crisis'. [Crisis being defined as overwhelming importance of an intolerable problem with feelings of hopelessness and helplessness resulting.]

She made an unsuccessful suicide attempt taking pills. She needed only one brush with death to completely restore her reality hold on life. [Moon/Jupiter/Saturn was there for her.]

There was a divorce and Jupiter transiting natal Jupiter/Saturn midpoint provided the substantial financial adjustment prelude to the divorce.

Interesting point - after the divorce Jack frequently visited the children. On one of his visits he and Laura got into a rather heated argument over the fact that he had not been to the dentist.

This incident was a familiar part of the twenty-five year marriage pattern that prompted the observation. Could Laura's MOON/JUPITER/SATURN possibly have been more of a mother to Jack when it could have been more of an understanding wife?

The confidential files have given you some valuable information in regard to the planets and suicide. Additional insights into suicide research have proved the following statements to be TRUE!

ALL "TRUE" STATEMENTS!

[1.] People that talk about committing suicide should be taken seriously. They are potential attempters1 TRUE

[2.] People who attempt suicide come from all walks of life. They do not fall in any distinct class or grouping. TRUE

[3.] Suicides do not happen without some warning! TRUE

[4.] People who are determined to commit suicide can be helped. TRUE

[5.] Never try to kid a person out of his suicide talk. TRUE

[6.] Once a person makes a suicide attempt he will not always be suicidal. TRUE

[7.] People who fail at a suicide attempt are a real threat to themselves. TRUE

[8.] Suicide does not run in families. TRUE

[9.] A suicide person is not a mentally-ill person. TRUE

[10.] Depression is usally a condition of a suicidal individual. TRUE

[11.] Depressed people often commit suicide when their symptoms seem to be improving. TRUE

[12.] More men than women commit suicide. TRUE

[13.] Women attempt suicide twice as often as men. TRUE

CHAPTER V

PLANETARY DEPRESSION/ANXIETY!

Recognize it! Then change it!

Prominent and dangerous depression and anxiety stages correlate with the planetary directions and transits contacting your natal chart.

It is vital for your security and happiness to recognize these depression/anxiety patterns in yourself as well as in others.

A whole new way of life will open up for you as you become aware of and are able to control your planetary behavioral responses.

Depression and anxiety can be described simplistically as states of melancholy, fear, apprehension or uncertainty; these states result from various ineffective emotional responses to the directions and transits of the planets.

The unfortunate emotional responses that create these unhappy states of depression and anxiety are simply a result of lack of understanding.

This 'lack of understanding' comes from not knowing how to benficially use the energies available through the planetary directions and transits contacting your natal chart.

This chapter is divided into three unique sections reflecting the building and combating stages of these states of depression and anxiety. These three sections are:

[1.] FEELINGS

A list of the life-denying, ineffective feelings that result from not understanding how to use planetary energies. [How to combat these negative feelings and create a beneficial situation is shown in the Keyword Clue Words section.]

[2.] WISDOM

In this section you will discover how to recognize depression/anxiety states through planetary behavioral pattern changes. You will then correlate these changes with two specific planets. Although behavior change patterns are affected by all the planets you will correlate these patterns using two specific planets only [Saturn and Neptune]. The purpose for using two specific planets is that by narrowing your field of planets it becomes easier for you to learn to identify 'behavior pattern changes' with 'planetary energies'.

As this process becomes learned you will then automatically apply this thinking to all of the planets. A sample of how you will apply this thinking to other planets will be given at the end of the Wisdom section.

[3.] KEYWORD CLUE WORDS

Learn how to use planetary energy effectively as an opportunity for you. Planetary Keyword Clue Words point the way to make things happen for you! Section I begins with FEELINGS.

FEELINGS - SECTION 1

FEELINGS - A list of the life-denying, ineffective feelings that result from not understanding how to use planetary energies.

Feelings are more than just contacts represented by the Moon. Although feeling involves the emotional part [MOON] of our nature there is an excited mental state of emotion that we experience as a result of our reaction to each planet's different energy.

All planets provoke some kind of 'feeling' response in us! Learning how to use this 'feeling' response is the path toward happiness and success in life. This chapter makes this potential happiness possible!

The slower moving, heavy planets are discussed only because of the obvious strength of influence of emotional response in the life!

These planets are: PLUTO - NEPTUNE - URANUS and SATURN.

PLUTO

Feelings of ISOLATION, ALIENATION and FANATICISM result from not understanding how to use Pluto's intensity effectively!

NEPTUNE

Feelings of HOPELESSNESS, DISSATISFACTION or ESCAPISM result from not understanding how to use Neptune's creativity effectively!

URANUS

Feelings of FRUSTRATION, INTOLERANCE and INCOMPATIBILITY result from not understanding how to use Uranus's 'uniqueness' for effective development.

SATURN

Feelings of LONELINESS, REJECTION or FAILURE result from not understanding how to use Saturn's discipline effectively.

WISDOM - SECTION II

Ineffective planetary feelings become obvious or are easily recognized through the manifestation of distinct patterns that exhibit definite behavior changes.

Your awareness development comes in two ways: first by reading and understanding a behavioral change pattern and secondly you will be further challenged as these behavioral change patterns are correlated with two specific planets - Saturn and Neptune. The FIVE BEHAVIORAL PATTERN CHANGES caused by planetary depression are:

[1.] <u>ENERGY PATTERN CHANGE</u>

The spirit or power to work and enjoy life changes; exhaustion versus hyper-active behavior can be either of two extreme energy-performance changes.

ENERGY DEPRESSION
<u>PLANETARY CORRELATION</u>

♄

Look for SATURN when depression slows down to an abnormal point.

♄

With Saturn directions or transits energy feelings can go from an emotional climate where the person is dull, languid, dispirited, and discouraged to an almost complete loss of interest in life!

♆

Look for Neptune when depression steps the energy up to a frantic state of activity

♆

Neptune speeds up the energy and maintains a surface hyper-active, inconsistent interest in life when depression changes the behavior.

Neptune is notoriously ambivalent. Expect the influence to be a co-existence of contradictory

♆

energy feelings about a person, object or action when Neptune contacts by direction or by transit.

[2.] CONCENTRATION PATTERN CHANGE

It takes great effort for the person to gather his thoughts; the mind works in a slow, labored manner.

Another depression reaction can manifest where concentration is dissipated by too much on the mind. The person is unable to completely follow through with thought patterns; apprehension and vague nebulous fears interfere with the successful mental thought.

CONCENTRATION DEPRESSION PLANETARY CORRELATION

♄

Look for Saturn influence when an individual's attention span is so difficult that simply collecting one's

♆

Neptune causes a person, when depressed, to talk in circles with the inability to spot or resolve the problem.

♄	♆
thoughts and directing them to an object becomes impossible	Animated discussions about feelings without gaining relief is typical Neptune depression.
This occurs at times when a person is speaking and just simply stops speaking with the inability to return to the train of thought.	Concentration can become an anxiety ridden preoccupation with future worry.
Concentration can also become a depressing preoccupation with past failures.	

[3.] <u>SELF ESTEEM PATTERN CHANGE</u>

The good opinion of one's self changes; the person no longer likes himself and feels a sense of worthlessness.

SELF ESTEEM DEPRESSION PLANETARY CORRELATION

♄

Saturn influence can make the person very pessimistic and negative in regard to the self.

The person affected by Saturn directions and transits can react ineffectively by either giving up on goals and aims in life or refusing to even set any goals in life for the self.

Saturn/MC contacts can create this condition through constant worry.

♆

Neptune influence brings anxiety and worry in regard to the ego or goals in life.

A condition of anxiety, worry and fear perpetuates a feeling of worthlessness.

The inability to feel secure in one's self esteem is typical of a Neptune MC influence.

There can be the anxious feeling that the ego is built on sand; no matter how rational the thinking tries to be there will be that subtle influence that makes a person feel good about the self one day and completely worthless the next day. Neptune/MC can create this condition.

[4.] SLEEP PATTERN CHANGE

Sleep habits can become extreme; either insomnia followed by pre-dawn wakening or increased need for an abnormal amount of sleep.

SLEEP PATTERN DEPRESSION PLANETARY CORRELATION

♄

The ineffectively influenced Saturn person always feels worse in the morning or after sleep. (This can indicate pessimistic thinking - dwelling on the self - before sleeping.)

The Saturn person will turn to anti-depressants to relieve depression.

♆

The ineffectively influenced Neptune person feels worse in the evening - feels better after sleep or rest. (Indication here is lack of moderation; energy wears down and person becomes confused and depressed.)

The Neptune influenced person turns to tranquilizers to relieve depression.

[5.] EATING PATTERN CHANGE

There is complete loss of interest in food or, at the other end of the continuum, will be the depressed, anxiety-ridden chronic eater.

EATING PATTERN DEPRESSION PLANETARY CORRELATION

♄	♆
Decreased appetite and weight loss will result from an ineffective response to a Saturn direction or transit.	A person who is suffering from depression through an ineffective response to Neptune will either eat constantly or intermittantly; no inbetween.
Constipation falls under Saturn influence; sometimes severe colitus condition.	Neptune depression creates the nervous snacker.
	Diarrhea falls under ineffective response to Neptune transits or directions.

You have just seen that with Saturn depression there is a isolated heaviness that actually drags the body down with its weight or melancholy feelings.

Saturn depression lowers the voice, impedes the circulation, weakens the faculties and makes communication of the problem impossible. You feel the weight of the planet!

With Neptune anxiety you see a subtle, undermining fear and apprehension that creates a nebulous type of doom in the offing.

The Neptune anxiety-ridden person at times can become immersed in an atmosphere of emotional paralysis from some unknown fear or confusion!

SUMMARY THOUGHT:
You have developed a new astro-psyche awareness in your reading to this point. As a result of this new awareness you can now easily recognize behavioral pattern changes that can occur through ineffective response to Saturn and Neptune.

Using KEYWORDS you will easily summarize the possible positive and negative manifestation with each planet.

You will carry this astro psyche awareness to the other planets. Uranus will bring change and in the negative frustration through change.

In the positive you have personal magnetism, genius, originality, individualism and self reliance affecting behavior. In the negative Uranus will be disruptive, hostile, and aggressive in behavior.

Ask yourself this question. How will Uranus 'sudden behavior change' affect energy patterns, concentration patterns, self esteem patterns, sleep and eating patterns? In the negative you are dealing with an extremely disruptive force.

Energy will be greatly increased. Since Uranus is genius ability there will be flashes of genius interrupting the concentration. Self esteem will be confident and strong. Sleep will definitely be disrupted. You will have insomnia to deal with, but also there will be a mental originality that cries for development during this insomnia period. Hurried disruptive eating patterns can be a result of Uranus. See how easily you can tie in behavior pattern changes with planetary energy!

Take the remaining planets and the principles or energies they represent and correlate them with the five behavioral pattern changes and see the interesting result.

To give you a start:
MOON brings feelings, emotions, moodiness and imagination to 1. Energy pattern 2. Concentration pattern 3. Self esteem pattern 4. Sleep pattern and 5. Eating pattern.

MERCURY brings mentality, communication, intellect and nervous reactions to the five pattern changes.

VENUS brings love, creativity, harmony, affection and pleasure to the five pattern changes. What will occur?

MARS represents energy, sex drive, action, ambition, desire and even violence. Great changes will occur in the five patterns!

JUPITER brings expansion, growth, sociability and wisdom to the five patterns: energy, concentration, self esteem, sleep and eating.

You have read interpretations for Saturn, Uranus and Neptune. Pluto will manifest as transformation (the ability to handle change). It will bring intensity, fanaticism, upheaval, elimination and regeneration of the five pattern changes. Start with the first pattern and ask yourself how will Pluto's principle affect this energy?

[1.] <u>Energy and Pluto?</u>
Intensely assertive or Fanatically belligerent

[2.] <u>Concentration and Pluto</u>?
Can be intensely analytical or or fanatically critical

[3.] <u>Self esteem and Pluto</u>?
Intensely directive or fanatically egotistical.

[4.] <u>Sleep and Pluto?</u>
Transforming - changes pattern
Intense need for sleep or fanatic insomnia

[5.] <u>Eating and Pluto?</u>
Transforming - Intense about eating patterns or fanatic urge for food or for abstinence (overweight or underweight).

KEYWORD CLUE WORDS - SECTION 3

Now you will learn how to use planetary energy effectively as an opportunity for you.

Planetary Keyword Clue Words point the way to make things happen for you!

First you will read a description of the planetary energy you must work with and secondly the KEYWORDS will show you how to use this energy.

The KEYWORD CLUE WORDS as to effective and ineffective action of certain planetary contacts show you how you can successfully <u>use</u> every direction and transit to your benefit through skillful manipulation of planetary energy!

Even with the difficult directions and transits, if you apply a 'never ceasing application' of energy toward the effective benefits, you can make them happen.

With the more difficult directions and transits there is more of a need for consistency of purpose to bring about beneficial results. Instead of depression, Saturn can be discipline. Instead of frustration, Uranus can be development. Instead of confusion and anxiety, Neptune can be creativity. Instead of isolation, Pluto can be transformation.

This points up the all-important fact: the planetary energies are there for your use. All you have to do is decide how you will react to these energies after you learn to understand them.

IMPORTANT!

THE KEYWORD PLANETARY CLUE WORDS apply not only to the natal planetary contacts but also to reactions occurring from direction and transit energy involving any of these same contacts.

For example SUN/PLUTO in the natal chart can be a power-hungry person. Likewise a person with a direction or transit of Pluto to his natal Sun can experience the force of a 'power hungry' urge during that period. The clue word will give you the ammunition necessary to make an opportunity for yourself out of the planetary energy available for your use!

USING SATURN'S PLANETARY ENERGY AS A BENEFIT FOR YOU!

Saturn's energy must have method and discipline or depression results. Saturn brings circumstances that you must conform with.

Concentration and application overcome oppression. Willpower and perseverance are developed.

Being forced to submit to circumstances forces a situation that no other planet creates. With Pluto you can throw out. With Uranus you can run. With Neptune you can become inactive and dream; but, with Saturn you either conform to what is available using what you have to work with or become deeply depressed.

Becoming depressed can include the following development of ineffective changes in your make-up. You become indifferent to your surroundings. Stimulation doesn't move you to any action. Even the simplest task can take great effort. Your reaction time is slowed up. Thinking becomes difficult. Days become an unending, life-denying eternity!

With the discipline possible here the self assertive and self expressive urge can produce industrious, successful people capable of shaping destinies! There is the ability to actually preserve life and health through this strong, potential for the devlopment of moderation.

Personal dignity, great respect and worldly success are possible for you by using Saturn's energy effectively!

SATURN KEYWORDS for NATAL CHART - TRANSITS or DIRECTIONS!	SATURN KEYWORD CLUE WORDS are DISCIPLINE or DEPRESSION - Take your choice!

SATURN/SUN	Disciplined or Depressed Individual Self Expression. This discipline or depression can come through the influence of a male.
SATURN/MOON	Disciplined or Depressed emotions. This discipline or depression can come through females, the family or the public.
SATURN/MERCURY	Disciplined or Depressed thinking or communication. This discipline or depression can come through the influence of a young person.
SATURN/VENUS	Disciplined or Depressed lovelife or creative life. This discipline or depression can come through the influence of the loved one.
SATURN/MARS	Disciplined or Depressed energy. This discipline or depression can come through male influence.
SATURN/JUPITER	Disciplined or Depressed opportunities (ways of expanding life). This discipline or depression can come through the influence of uncles, parents or authority figures.

SATURN/URANUS	Disciplined or Depressed development. Depression comes from refusing to change. Change can be development at certain times in the life.
SATURN/NEPTUNE	Disciplined or Depressed creativity. Structure comes to creativity. Not accepting the Saturn concentration and application creates depression and anxiety for the Neptune sensitivity. The Neptune sensitivity is the creative side of the make-up.
SATURN/PLUTO	Disciplined or Depressed transformations. Sometimes separation must be accepted as a necessary part of life.
SATURN/ASC	Disciplined or Depressed outlook and environment. Without discipline you permit someone in your environment to cause you depression.
SATURN/MC	Disciplined or Depressed Ego and goals in life. You can permit false duty to hold you back in life. This false duty can come through the family or colleagues.

SATURN/NODE — Disciplined or Depressed contacts. You permit friends or acquaintances to stifle or oppress you.

USING URANUS'S PLANETARY ENERGY AS A BENEFIT FOR YOU!

Uranus can be your greatest developer or your greatest frustrator. The unexpected elements in the nature of strong-willed Uranus brings an energy that forces change; this of course occurs when a Uranus transit or direction contacts your chart. This energy forces the chart to grow and develop suddenly!

Sudden Uranus energy unfolds, part by part, the potential of the individual and advances him from one stage to another stage.

When this Uranian energy erupts and development is prevented from taking place frustration results. This Uranus frustration is merely the result of the inability of a force to develop. If the individual is not prepared to use this energy a psychological state of conflict is created.

Although frustration and conflict are part of every-day occurrence in life the adjustment to strong-will Uranus frustration can be so dynamic that the energy either develops or destroys the individual.

Reaction to Uranus frustration and conflict motivates one toward activity to reduce or eliminate the discomfort; thus the Uranus adjustment process.

Planetary development or frustration can involve a 'fight' or a 'flight'. A fight example of a consciously experienced Uranus transit or direction could be a disciplined fight for development. This would be a Saturn/ Uranus contact.

A subconscious Uranus 'fight' or 'flight' could be a Uranus/Neptune contact where the action involves development and the individual actually takes flight or runs through trips and vacations from the work involved developing the creativity.

Now - discover the unique ways in which Uranus can develop you or frustrate you.

Since you have become familiar with the basic Keyword Interpretation through the Saturn keywords we will develop the interpretation more.

URANUS KEYWORDS FOR NATAL CHART - TRANSITS or DIRECTIONS!	URANUS KEYWORD CLUE WORDS are DEVELOPMENT or FRUSTRATION Take your choice!
URANUS/SUN	Developed or Frustrated individual self expression. This development or frustration can come through a male.

[*Uranus/Sun*]
Opportunity for the development of the individual self expression if the lifestyle has been stable and disciplined. Uranus brings leadership and independence to the development. When the individual is not discipline and prepared for this sudden change, with strength of character, then the result can be eccentricity, stubbornness or peculiarity. Acute frustration then leads to disruption and discord.

URANUS/MOON	Developed or Frustrated emotions or feelings. This development or frustration can come through a female, the family or the public.

[*Uranus/Moon*]
Opportunity for the emotions to develop a 'uniqueness' along with intuitive strength. This requires a development involving progressive feelings. Frustration results when nervous ten-

sion from self will causes upsets with others not quite as progressive in their thinking as the Uranus/Moon individual.

URANUS/MERCURY Developed or Frustrated thinking and communication. Obstinacy contributes to this frustration. This development or frustration can come through a young person.

[Uranus/Mercury]

Opportunity for the thinking and communication to develop suddenly and uniquely along very original lines. Frustration occurs from the unpopularity this 'differentness' has with others. Private study for mental development or being with those of like Uranus thinking can offset nervous tension.

URANUS/VENUS Developed or Frustralovelife or creative life. This development or frustration can come through the influence of the loved one.

[Uranus/Venus]

Opportunity for the love or creative principle to develop; effectively this will add a note of excitement to a stable love union or a certain 'uniqueness' to artistic endeavors. Nervous instability from keeping strong, repressed desires in control results in painful emotional frustration. Creative outlet here is much desired.

URANUS/MARS — Developed or Frustrated energy. A male can develop or influence your energy under Uranus/Mars.

[*Uranus/Mars*]
Opportunity to develop a new aggressive dominant forceful energy. Leadership will play a part in this development; temper and erratic behavior lead to frustration of the strong, original energy.

URANUS/JUPITER — Developed or Frustrated opportunities or ways of opening up life.

[*Uranus/Jupiter*]
Opportunity to develop using energy that provides growth through mental power and originality. Frustration will naturually come from arrogant, rebellious or wasteful behavior which is the other side of the coin.

URANUS/SATURN — Developed or Frustrated discipline. This development or frustration can come through authority figures.

[*Uranus/Saturn*]
Opportunity to acquire beneficial

disciplined development in some area of life. Routine, method and hard work will offset inevitable frustration from stubbornness or eccentricity from this energy.

URANUS/NEPTUNE Developed or Frustrated sensitivity or creativity. You can permit confusion through improper placing of limits.

[*Uranus/Neptune*]
Opportunity to develop the unique combination of practical vision and idealism. Routing and structure make this possible. Emotional eccentricity and confusion bring frustration.

URANUS/PLUTO Developed or Frustrated transformations. You permit 'change' without enough consideration.

[*Uranus/Pluto*]
Opportunity for development through transformation. Beneficial regeneration of ideas and lifestyle involves discipline. Restlessness brings wasted energy and inevitable frustration.

URANUS/ASC Developed or Frustrated outlook and environment. You permit someone in your environment to develop or frustrate you.

[Uranus/Ascendant]

Opportunity to develop unique, progressive thinking and an original environment. Without discipline the outlook can become revolutionary and bizarre creating disruption in the environment that is upsetting to all. Frustration will be the inevitable result. Someone in the environment can be a strong developing influence or a strong frustrating influence.

URANUS/MC	Developed or Frustrated Ego and life goals. With this combination you can permit a poor, sudden-career change.

[Uranus/MC]

Opportunity to develop a new career or a progressive line of thought in the career. It is a chance to develop exceptional talent in the profession.

URANUS/NODE	Developed or Frustrated contacts. You can permit friends or acquaintances to bring 'too much' change into your life.

[Uranus/Node]

Opportunity to meet and develop very unique relationships. These contacts will in some way stimulate your own originality.

USING NEPTUNE'S PLANETARY ENERGY AS A BENEFIT FOR YOU!

Neptune's energy must have a creative outlet; it must be able to hope, anticipate and dream in some way or it becomes panic and anxiety.

Neptune's rays are so subtle that you can be immersed in Neptune confusion and not know it. It is most important to recognize the ineffective Neptune signs calling for re-creation of the Neptune energy.

Nervous fatigues is a sign of Neptune energy reacting ineffectively. Your normal, healthy daily living patterns are being sabotaged in some way. This can include disruption of your sleep pattern, exercise outlet or mealtime harmony. In short Neptune can easily undermine the balance in life.

Preoccupation with fears and panic tied in with the need for security can be another manifestation of ineffective Neptune energy. These Neptune anxiety states can result in psychosomatic symptoms such as air hunger, pressure in the chest, ulcers, allergies, or even a flight instinct from a particular person. Neptune brings physical ailments that are hard to diagnose as a result of its subtle, undermining influence.

Once you recognize any of the above Neptune aspects in your life then you must ask yourself an important question. Question: When I become the most upset who have I just talked with? The amount of time you spend with a person is inconsequential in detecting the 'Neptune anxiety factor'. When you discover the person that prevents you from controlling an 'anxiety' reaction to this person then you must do something concrete in regard to this relationship. This person must be limited, controlled or possibly avoided completely in order to change this unhappy Neptune condition.

Strong Neptune contacts in charts give tremendous creative energy. This energy demands an outlet. The creative need can be satisfied through walks, music or artistic hobbies including painting, dancing, singing, or writing. This high creative potential demands more rest than another chart without a Neptune emphasis. Since creativity is necessary to offset Neptune anxiety, discover how you can 'use' Neptune for your benefit!

NEPTUNE KEYWORDS FOR NATAL CHART - TRANSITS or DIRECTIONS	NEPTUNE KEYWORD CLUE WORDS are CREATIVITY or ANXIETY Take your choice!
NEPTUNE/SUN	Sensitive Individual Self

Expression must become Creative in some way or individual becomes Anxiety prone. A male influence can build this creativity or anxiety.

[*Neptune/Sun*]
Opportunity for high-strung, anxious Neptune individual to learn to develop the creative or spiritual side of the make-up. This automatically offsets worry, delusion, anxiety and easy influencing of others.

NEPTUNE/MOON Sensitive Feelings and Emotions must have a creative outlet or they become anxious, fear ridden and panicky.

[*Neptune/Moon*]
Opportunity for inspirational feelings to be developed and manifest reality emotions as a result of this direction or transit. Glamour or dreamy feelings that lead to escapism will disappear along with anxiety feelings resulting from this misplaced emotional idealism. A female, the family or the public (Moon) may have an influence here.

NEPTUNE/MERCURY Sensitive mind must have a creative outlet or thinking becomes anxious and insecure.

[*Neptune/Mercury*]
Opportunity for heightened sensitive

thinking to work toward organization, objectivity and clear communication with others. Delicate, acute mental senses can generate cunning and deceptive behavior when the spiritual element is not incorporated into the thinking (Mercury).

NEPTUNE/VENUS   Sensitive lovelife and artistic life must have a creative outlet or love becomes anxious and insecure.

[Neptune/Venus]

Opportunity for the love nature to seek idealism through a deep emotional spiritual rapport with the partner. Compassion and understanding must take presidence over romance, dreaming and sensualism for emotional fulfillment. Anxiety results from non-durable love.

NEPTUNE/MARS   Energy must be creative in some way or it becomes anxious and insecure. Analytical ability is strong. A male can be an intellectual influence or an anxiety influence.

[Neptune/Mars]

Opportunity for energy to become effective by seeking spiritual orientation, practical helpfulness and mental contol. Ineffectively Neptune/Mars will pull toward confused mental energy and a sensual, carnal state.

NEPTUNE/JUPITER Opportunities that are spiritual and creative or insecure and unstable. To receive benefit from the opportunities offered under Ne/Ju there must be caution.

[*Neptune/Jupiter*]

Opportunity for expansion of an extremely idealistic nature through spiritual goals incorporated with strong, realistic limits. Losing contact with reality and living in a world of private fantasy is possible when Neptune over-rides Jupiter!

NEPTUNE/SATURN Sensitivity must be spiritual and creative to satisfy Saturn reality. Anxiety results when Neptune's sensitivity does not maintain Saturn structure. Confusion can occur through authority figures. There are times when their ideas of discipline become out-dated.

[*Neptune/Saturn*]

Opportunity for the creation of a strong Neptune/Saturn combination: spiritual energy with practical discipline. Saturn will be wholesome and enduring and Neptune practical and idealistic. Ineffectively a subtle, selfish cunning with cruel undercurrents can develop.

NEPTUNE/URANUS Development must be creative and spiritual or it becomes insecure and anxious.

[*Neptune/Uranus*]

Opportunity for change or spiritual development that relieves anxiety. Creative development keeps Ne/Ur from becoming erratic or escapist in its manifestation.

NEPTUNE/PLUTO Transformations that must be viewed through a spiritual outlook. The change will ofset an anxious intensity of mind.

[*Neptune/Pluto*]

Opportunity for sensitivity to become practical and useful. Without structure Neptune can become undermining and confusing and Pluto can become fanatic. Intense creativity can be effective with Ne/Pl contacts.

NEPTUNE/ASC Outlook must become creative and spiritual in order to offset confusion and anxiety. Someone in the environment can be a strong creative or anxiety influence.

[*Neptune/Asc*]

Opportunity for the development of a

practical, spiritual outlook and a tranquil environment resulting from routine and method that offsets anxiety. Outlook and environment will be spiritual or worrisome.

NEPTUNE/MC Ego and goals in life will have a spiritual orientation or a feeling of unfullment results.

[*Neptune/MC*]
Opportunity for lofty goals to have a practical creative or spiritual factor. Corruption and deception can come to this contact and create strange undermining conditions unless goals in life are honest and above board.

NEPTUNE/NODE Contacts or associations will be creative and spiritually oriented or undermining and confused.

[*Neptune/Node*]
Opportunity to make friends or acquaintances with a spiritual make-up or a creative make-up. Ineffectively contacts can be confusing, cunning or undermining in some way. These associations can bring anxiety into the life.

USING PLUTO'S PLANETARY ENERGY AS A BENEFIT FOR YOU!

Pluto is transformation. Transformation simply means 'changing the form.

Pluto brings the energies that eliminate old conditions and regenerate or cause new conditions to be born again. This is the natural Pluto transforming process.

When this transforming occurs in your chart you must make adjustments and change your views: status quo is no longer workable.

Pluto is the planet of self rediscovery!

When you have a Pluto transit or direction and you do not change with its transforming energy you become isolated with the old condition. 'Holding on' to old conditions is no longer satisfactory.

Using Pluto's intense transforming energy effectively will bring you new and better ways of living. See the following dynamic ways in which this is accomplished.

PLUTO KEYWORD CLUE WORDS are TRANSFORMATION or ISOLATION -
Take your choice!

PLUTO/SUN

Individual self expression encounters

transformation or isolation!

Opportunity now for you to bring into existence new dominant facets of your individual self expression. An enormous amount of energy is now at your disposal to change beneficially your individual self expression. You can do this by leaving old attitudes and habits behind.

This new development can come through the acceptance of leadership and power in some area of your life; this will involve discipline of these Pluto energies. Arrogance and fanaticism at this time will force you into isolation.

A male [SUN] figure can play a part in this transforming process; therefore be aware of any new attitudes you accept through male influence. These new attitudes can re-create or isolate your self expression.

PLUTO/MOON

Feelings encounter transformation or isolation!

Opportunity for your emotions and feelings to be re-created with more depth and perspective. Heightened sensitivity can help point the way to understanding how your emotional needs can be better satisfied and will thus react with more harmony and satisfaction.

This contact demands successful co-operation between the 'will' and the 'imagination' along with more practical sense in the emotional life.

The emotional influence is extremely strong. Isolation can result from forcing actions and relationships with others.

A female, the family or the public can play a part in this transforming process; therefore be aware of any new emotions or feelings that lead to major changes. Weigh the new feeling decision against the quality of the person influencing you.

PLUTO/MERCURY

Thinking and Communication encounter transformation or isolation!

Opportunity for the mind to be released of the past through new thought processes and beneficial ways of accepting the past.

The intellect now has the power and the intensity to probe deeply and successfully into any field. Thus there is enormous intellectual influence for you at this time through writing, teaching or just plain communicating in your sphere of life.

You bring on your own mental isolation if you refuse to let the mind caste off old, out-dated thinking. This would happen by staying obsessed with your old ideas and thought patterns. Intense communicative irritation is a signal you are not moving in the right direction.

Extremist attitudes can develop. Two attitudes that will isolate you at this time are (1.) inability to be open to another's opinions or (2.) accepting mental manipulation by another.

<u>PLUTO/VENUS</u>

Love and creative potential encounter transformation or isolation!

<u>Opportunity</u> for you to transform your old love concepts. A love relationship can now be renewed or restored in some way. Being rigid with a loved one brings emotional isolation.

The love relationship can experience a 'born again' quality or there can be an emotional self sufficiency created through universal love.

The creative potential can re-create itself and find dramatic new avenues of beneficial expression. There is now available powerful creative energy for your use. With discipline this creativity can tie in with scientific ability.

The loved one can play a part in this transforming process; therefore be aware of any new love attitudes that lead to major relationship changes. Do the new love ideas have quality that will add to the union?

PLUTO/MARS

Energy encounters transformation or isolation!

Opportunity for you to transform or experience the process of regeneration in regard to your energy.

You now have a dynamic surplus of power and force available to you; this force or intensity of vigor rushes through you and forces new outlets or new ways of moving forward or energizing your life.

New energy channels create new and better performance by bringing new conditions of life into focus.

If this energy does not perform its transforming function now it will be turned inward upon the individual. The intensity of this inward flow not only isolates the individual but victimizes him with great new tension problems.

A male can play a part in this energy re-creation process. Be aware of any new action resulting from male influence. Ask yourself, 'How is this influence changing my energy?'

PLUTO/JUPITER

Opportunities encounter transformations or isolation!

Opportunity for a change in the condition, nature or character of your usual ways of expanding life and creating opportunities. This new energy brings a good change for self-advancement and the development of power.

If you do not permit this transforming

energy to take place opportunity becomes isolated. You are wise to accept the new Pluto way of expanding life and using opportunity. This decision can offset 'aloneness' or the absence of a path of expansion.

Since Jupiter represents a male in the 50's as well as the 'uncle' there will be a possible influence through either. Look for this influence and analyze it for benefits for you.

PLUTO/SATURN

Discipline encounters transformation or isolation!

Opportunity for a change in your 'structured' way of doing things. Saturn represents discipline, structure or 'lack'. Pluto is intensity and transformation. Look for life to encounter a change in the rigid habit patterns you have built through the years. This change will fill the 'lack' that has occurred through this disciplined intensity!

You can now bring intensity and purpose together and develop something of quality in your life. Here the new form that is created will be a result of Pluto's intensity pushing

Saturn's structure for a new method.

EXAMPLE: A great change in a relationship as a result of a long separation. Divorce can also occur.

This contact will demand stamina and hard work to create the effective transformation it now seeks. There will be a certain amount of isolation even in the effective manifestation due to the extreme hard work necessary to make this transformation possible.

Jealousy or vindictiveness due to the blocking of personal ambition through one's own inability to master the situation can result in isolation. Athority figures can influence at this time.

PLUTO/URANUS

Development encounters transformation or isolation!

Opportunity for growth or advancement through progressive change. This is a time when Pluto will bring a strength of will power that rises to the progressive needs of the individual.

Change [Uranus] will occur through the Pluto willpower — transformation. Others may assist you in the creation of this change.

At times there can be drastic upheavals through Pluto/Uranus. This involves a much greater adjustment but in the long run the Pluto transformation still will have been a benefit in the development (Uranus).

PLUTO/NEPTUNE

Development encounters creativity or anxiety.

Opportunity for the creative potential to expand in an effective, beneficial intense way. Intense sensitivity demands a creative outlet for the tricky handling of this energy combination - Pluto/Neptune.

Will power combines with the highly creative imagination and with discipline produces great artistic works. Channelling this creative intensity through structure is a must; mass confusion can be the result of permitting this dynamic energy to operate without limits.

Neptune's restlessness can be harnessed through Pluto's strong transforming willpower. There can be great advancement through the regeneration (Pluto) of the mental (Neptune) strength.

It is important that travel, at this

time, have a purpose. Nothing can be effective with this combination of energies unless there is some structure. [KEYWORDS: Pluto/Transformation - Neptune/Creativity and Saturn/Structure. The secret of making the Pluto/Neptune is of course through Saturn structure!)

PLUTO/ASCENDANT

The outlook and the environment encounter transformation or isolation!

Opportunity for you to have a complete metamorphosis in your outlook which would be your mental view of things. This complete change will also occur in your environment; by environment is meant 'what surrounds you'.

At this time the personality as well as the conditions within the environment need regeneration or the capacity to 'produce anew'. The way of thinking plus what surrounds you has become outdated; it can no longer exist as is.

Holding on to old outlooks as well as to old unsatisfactory environmental conditions will bring strong isolation.

This can happen to you psychologically from what has occurred previously. An example of this could be 'change' as a result of another's actions effecting your thinking. The other's actions being of course the motive that caused the change. This way Pluto can transform through someone within your environment. At this time environmental change must be adjusted to; progress, not isolation will then be the effective result.

PLUTO/MC

The Ego and the life goals encounter transformation or isolation!

Opportunity for the Ego, or the self as distinguished from any other self, to reproduce anew. This Ego part of you that results from experiences and reactions to the outside world must go through a transforming process.

The aims and goals in life will be seriously considered as a result of previous interaction with others or events. As a result of this regeneration thinking will change. Pluto's transformation is the culmination of a long, time period; what erupts now has been in process for many, many months.

If the Ego and the goals in life cannot rebuild then the out-dated Ego and life goals will destroy the self esteem and bring a sense of isolation. It is time for career progress.

Pluto/MC can represent female influence; be aware of domination through the female.

PLUTO/NODE

The contacts undergo a transformation.

Opportunity for your relationships to be transformed; this can be a change in nature or disposition in you or in your contacts. [Contacts can be friends, acquaintances or lovers.]

Since Pluto develops what has been hidden for a long time its contact with the Node can completely regenerate a relationship. EXAMPLE: Certain attitudes and concepts are revealed through an old friend that you had never been aware of as part of the friend's make-up. These attitudes and concepts are unique and take some adjusting to on your part.

Pluto/Node can also bring separation and then reappearance of a once-intimate contact. If there is a long time span since contact with this person the relationship will undoubtedly involve some transformation.

Isolation results if an individual does not make relationship adjustments and choses to caste them off. Again you must co-operate with Pluto's transforming principle.

GLOSSARY

<u>ASTROLOGY</u> - Astrology is the relationship between the celestial bodies and the earth as it relates to human behavior. Astrology can be divided into four main classifications: [1.] Planets [2.] Zodiac [3.] Houses and [4.] Aspects.

<u>COSMOBIOLOGY</u> - Cosmobiology is a scientific discipline that uses the 90 degree circle as an instrument to study the influence of the positions of the stellar bodies on human behavior and to give interpretation to guide human behavior accordingly. Reinhold Ebertin is the founder of Cosmobiology.

D.F.ASTROL.S. - D.F.Astrol.S. stands for 'Diploma from the Faculty of Astrological Studies' in England. The diploma of this internationally renowned course of study is given at the end of an extensive period of study taking at the miniumum two years to complete. The late Charles E. O. Carter, well-published scholar whose work followed that of the late Alan Leo, was President of The Faculty of Astrological Studies in England. The 'Roy Allin' award is an international award given the student who excels in interpretation. Karen Ober Savalan, author of this book is holder of this award.

DIRECTIONS - A degree for a year. When we use the term directions we are generally referring to Solar Arc directions which is the specific calculation in regard to the daily motion of the Sun. Specifically the term, 'direction' is used to refer to the movement of two or more stellar bodies within the horoscope (360° circle) or the Unigram (90° circle). See definition of the term 'Unigram'.

MIDPOINT - A midpoint is a mathematical point halfway between two stellar bodies that tells the interpretative picture.

MIDPOINT AUTHORS:

EBERTIN, REINHOLD _ Reinhold Ebertin is a European scholar and founder of the scientific discipline, cosmobiology. Astrology students can benefit from Reinhold Ebertin's book, "The Combination of Stellar Influences".

WITTE-LEFELDT - Alfred Witte is the European scholar who originated the midpoint theory. Astrology students can benefit from Alfred Witte and Hermann Lefeldt's book, "Rules For Planetary-Pictures".

SAVALAN, KAREN OBER - Karen Ober Savalan is an American scholar and founder of the scientific for, 'The Unigram' explained in this glossary.

Karen Ober Savalan is the author of MIDPOINT INTERPRETATION SIMPLIFIED - MIDPOINT SYNASTRY SIMPLIFIED - MIDPOINT LOVE SIMPLIFIED - LOVE-ANGER and KAREN'S KEYWORD COMPENDIUM [Books published by American Federation of Astrologers - P.O. Box 22040 - Tempe Arizona 85282 - U.S.A.].

STRUCTURE - The midpoint structure is referred to as a 'tree' because it is composed of limbs which are the midpoints with a main stellar body at the top of the tree. At times the structure gives a planetary picture of the main stellar body in question. Following is an illustration of the structure of Mars Midpoint Structure.

TRANSIT - The passage of a planet over the place or longitude of an important position in the natal or horoscope of direction.

UNIGRAM - A systematic, logical and ingenious, 'one page' form that unites all the principles of traditional astrology plus all the principles of modern midpoints. The UNIGRAM was invented and copyrighted exclusively by the Author, Karen Ober Savalan - D.F.Astrol.S.

WHAT THE UNIGRAM OFFERS YOU !!!

[1.] A complete, professional life-study of an individual on one page! [Size 8-1/2 x 14 inches!]
[2.] Ingenious form that unites all the principles of traditional Astrology and modern Midpoints!
[3.] Enables you to use your 'favorite' house system with your Ascendant on the left just as in your traditional chart!
[4.] Unites 4 forms into one unique form! The 4 forms are:
  [1.] 360° Circle - Astrology
  [2.] 90° Circle - Midpoints
  [3.] Astrological aspect table
  [4.] Midpoint structure
[5.] See - at a glance - all the directions and transits in the 360° circle and the 90° circle!
[6.] Perfect organization - no more messy files! Pull only one form for a complete case study!

ASCENDANT AND ITS PLACE IN THE UNIGRAM

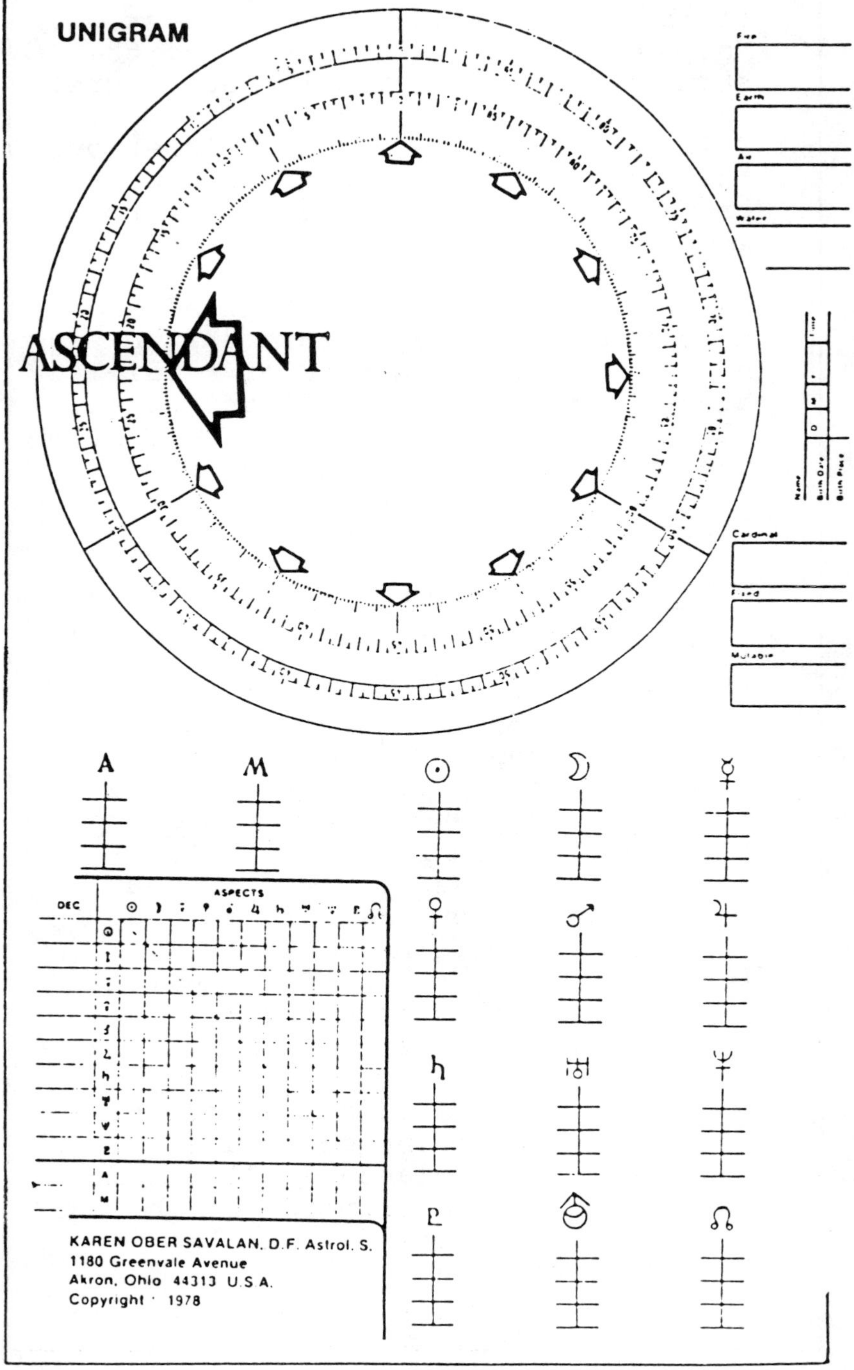

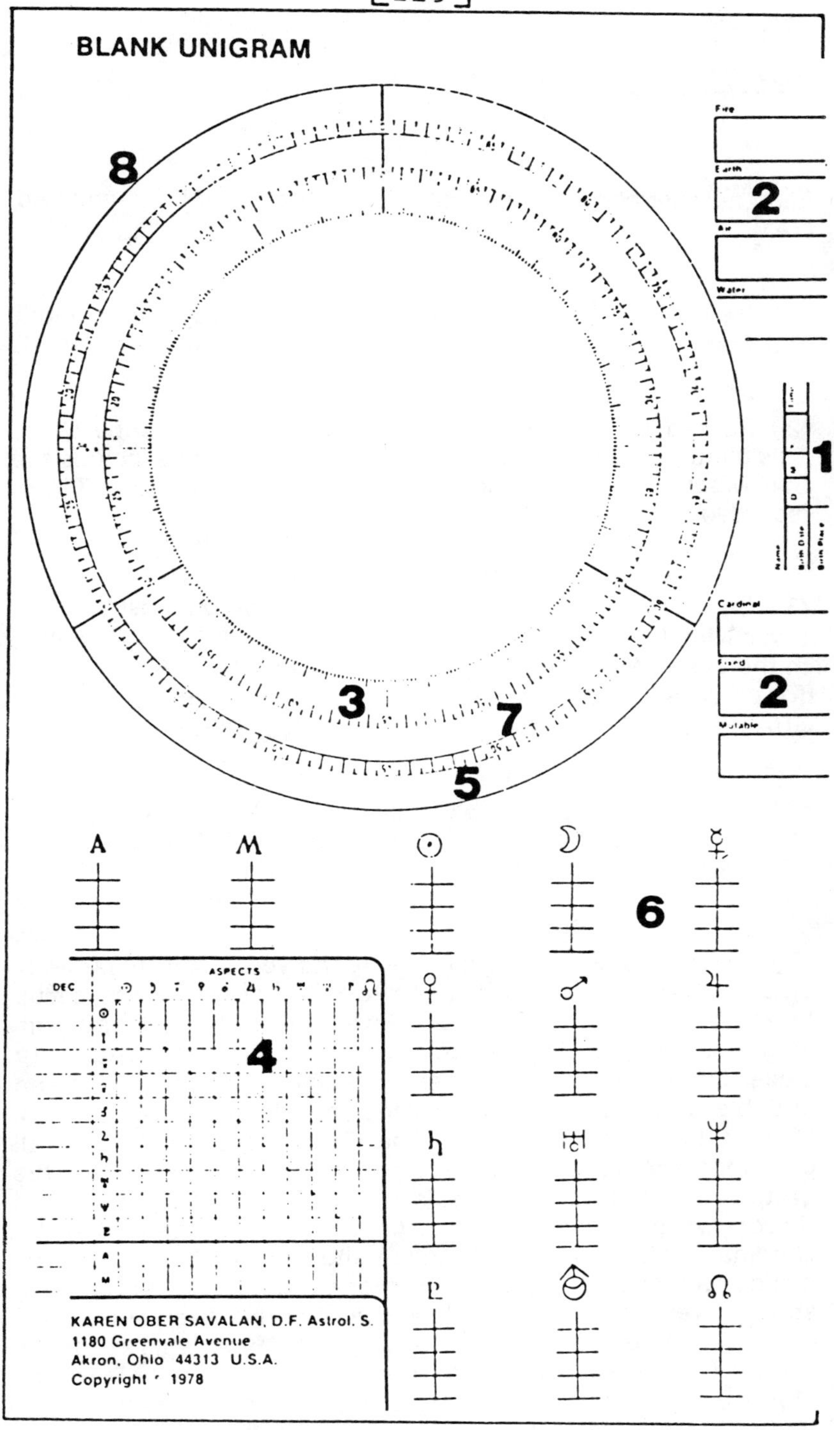
BLANK UNIGRAM
8
Fire
Earth
2
Air
Water
1
Name
Birth Date
Birth Place
Cardinal
Fixed
2
Mutable
3
7
5
A
M
6
ASPECTS
DEC
4
A
M
KAREN OBER SAVALAN, D.F. Astrol. S.
1180 Greenvale Avenue
Akron, Ohio 44313 U.S.A.
Copyright © 1978

HOW TO SET UP THE UNIGRAM

Each number corresponds with the explanation of the numbered area.

(1.) Record the name of the chart. Record the day, time, month and year of birth of the chart in the UNIGRAM section marked #1.

(2.) Record all the Quadruplicities and Triplicities in the chart. This includes all the stellar bodies. The stellar bodies include the Sun, Moon, Planets, Ascendant, M.C. and the Moon's Node. This is recorded in the UNIGRAM section marked #2.

(3.) Set up your 360 degree circle, your traditional astrological circle with the Ascendant on the left as you are used to calculating in the past. (We are taking for granted your preliminary calculations have already been completed.) This is recorded in the UNIGRAM section marked #3.

(4.) Set up your Aspect Table showing all the calculated aspects in your 360 degree circle. This is recorded in the UNIGRAM section marked #4.

(5.) Set up your 90 degree circle entering your natal stellar body placements only in this 90 degree circle. On a scrap of paper set up three groups entitled: Cardinal - Fixed and Mutable. Copy from your standard 360 degree circle (traditional horoscope) all your stellar bodies into the proper group entitled: Cardinal, Fixed and Mutable. The Cardinal group will include all placements in Aries, Cancer, Libra and Capricorn. The Fixed group will include all placements in Taurus, Leo, Scorpio and Aquarius. The Mutable group will include all placements in Gemini, Virgo, Sagittarius and Pisces. On the cosmogram put pencil marks at the end of the Cardinal section, the Fixed section and the Mutable section. To distinguish the Quadruplicities from one another for the beginning student we use colors. The following coloring has been established as representing each Quadruplicity. Blue is used for the Cardinal signs. Red is used for the Fixed signs. Green is for the Mutable signs. In the beginning use pencil to enter your stellar bodies because of mistakes.

Next transfer all the 13 stellar bodies from the piece of scrap paper to the 90 degree circle. Begin with 0 - 30 degrees of the Cardinal section. Continue counter-clockwise until you have finished the entire 90 degree circle. When you are finished you will have completed your Cardinal, Fixed and Mutable section.

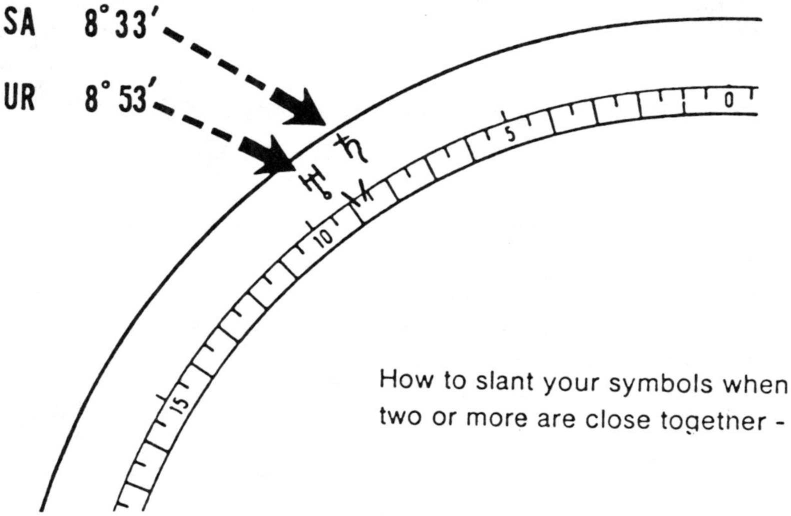

How to slant your symbols when two or more are close together -

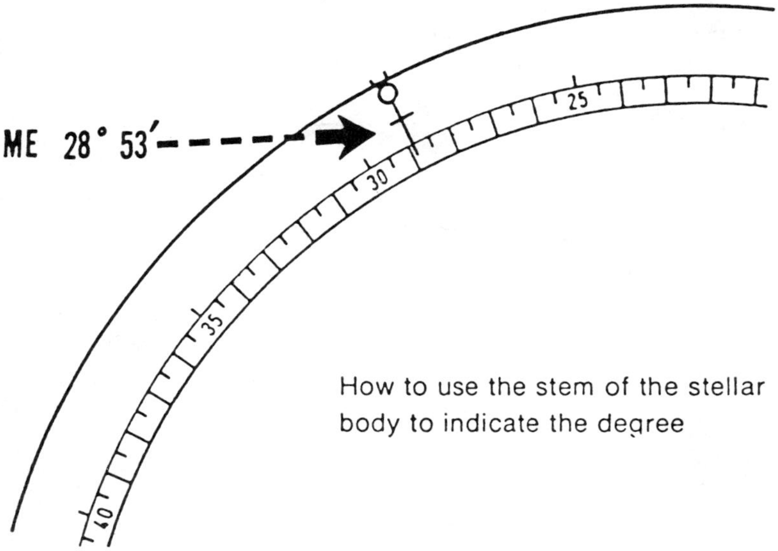

How to use the stem of the stellar body to indicate the degree

(6.) Calculate all your midpoints for your stellar bodies and enter these in the correct midpoint structure.

(7.) **Forecasting** - There are two 90 degree circles in the UNIGRAM. The larger outside 90 degree circle is for recording the natal stellar bodies. The smaller 90 degree circle will be used in your study of directions because this circle - being on top - can be rotated easily.

(8.) **Forecasting** - Enter your current Transits

BIBLIOGRAPHY

The Rulership Book by Rex Bills

Astrology and The Abnormal Mind by Dr. Wm. J. Tucker

The Will To Live by Arnold A. Hutschnecker MD

Anatomy Of An Illness by Norman Cousins

Mind As Healer, Mind As Slayer by Kenneth R. Pelletier

Mental Health Through Will Training by Abraham A. Low

The Secret Of Instantaneous Healing by Harry Douglas Smith

How To Use Auto Suggestion Effectively by John Duckworth

A New Guilde To Rational Living by Albert Ellis Ph D and Robert A. Harper Ph D

The Art Of Selfishness by David Seabury

Reason And Emotion In Psychotherapy by Albert Ellis

The Angry Book By Theodore Isaac Rubin MC

Love And Will By Rollo May

An Encyclopedial Of Psychological Astrology By C.E.O. Carter B.A.

ILLUSTRATION INDEX

PAGE